Further Praise for *Know-It-All Society*

"The book is accessible, admirably concise, clearly written, and richly insightful, both as a cultural diagnosis and as an exemplar of applying philosophical inquiry—ancient or otherwise—to everyday problems."   —*Booklist*

"[Michael Patrick] Lynch offers an insightful, timely message."
                                                                —*Kirkus Reviews*

"This book is both a treasure and a treat—that rare volume that is philosophically rich, politically relevant, and lyrically written."
            —Eboo Patel, author of *Out of Many Faiths*

"A sharp and engaging critique of the tribal arrogance that's so common in contemporary life, by one of our leading public philosophers. Michael Patrick Lynch has a lot of provocative ideas—about social media, the rise of Donald Trump, whether we have to listen to neo-Nazis, and much else—and his rich book is a delight to engage with."
            —Paul Bloom, professor of psychology, Yale University, and author of
                    Against Empathy: The Case for Rational Compassion

"Michael Patrick Lynch has done it. Finally, someone has answered the question that has exasperated so many in this 'post-truth' era: Why are some people unconvinced by facts? The answer lies not in irrationality but identity. In these polarized times, to question someone's beliefs is to question their sense of self. In this book, Lynch brilliantly demonstrates that a solution to the problem of belief lies not just in valuing truth and evidence but in reforming some of the toxic mental attitudes that exist not just in others but in ourselves."
            —Lee McIntyre, author of *The Scientific Attitude*

"In this important volume Michael Patrick Lynch turns his attention to an important source of contemporary political tribalism: arrogant overconfidence. He presents a clearheaded diagnosis of the ills that befall societies that are dominated by those who think that they know it all, and he makes a compelling case for the importance of truth and humility in the struggle to create a new, more open-minded political culture. This book embodies all the qualities of public philosophy at its best. It is rigorous, thought-provoking, and engaging. A must-read for anyone who cares about the future of democracy."

—Alessandra Tanesini, Cardiff University

"A timely book on an important topic in our political culture today. Michael Patrick Lynch is just the person to bring philosophical insight to these challenges—of trust, expertise, disagreement, and the prospects for conversation across the deep political chasms of our day."

—Sanford C. Goldberg, author of *To the Best of Our Knowledge*

"If we have learned anything over these past few years, it is that democracy is difficult. In this essential book for our times, Michael Patrick Lynch unflinchingly lays out its central conundrums in painfully recognizable ways, and bravely offers hope and, perhaps, some ways out. A remarkable achievement."

—Jason Stanley, author of *How Fascism Works*

"Michael Patrick Lynch's book uses the classics of philosophy to examine why our society, in a modern age of technology and education, is increasingly centered around a dysfunctional, narcissistic rejection of objectivity and reason. *Know-It-All Society* challenges us to consider why we arrogantly refuse to listen to each other, no matter what our politics or our beliefs."

—Tom Nichols, author of *The Death of Expertise*

"Professor Lynch not only diagnoses the reasons for our current predicament, but also suggests ways in which we can begin to challenge our tribal arrogance. *Know-It-All Society* is an important (and wonderfully readable) book."

—David Edmonds, host of BBC's *The Big Idea*

KNOW-IT-ALL
SOCIETY

Truth and Arrogance in Political Culture

Michael Patrick Lynch

LIVERIGHT PUBLISHING CORPORATION

A DIVISION OF W. W. NORTON & COMPANY

INDEPENDENT PUBLISHERS SINCE 1923

For information about permission to reproduce selections from this book,
write to Permissions, Liveright Publishing Corporation, a division of
W. W. Norton & Company, Inc., 500 Fifth Avenue, New York, NY 10110

For information about special discounts for bulk purchases, please contact
W. W. Norton Special Sales at specialsales@wwnorton.com or 800-233-4830

Manufacturing by LSC Communications
Book design by Daniel Lagin
Production manager: Beth Steidle

Library of Congress Cataloging-in-Publication Data

Names: Lynch, Michael P. (Michael Patrick), 1966– author.
Title: Know-it-all society : truth and arrogance in political culture /
Michael Patrick Lynch.
Description: First Edition. | New York : Liveright Publishing Corporation, 2019. |
Includes bibliographical references and index.
Identifiers: LCCN 2019014604 | ISBN 9781631493614 (hardcover)
Subjects: LCSH: Information society—Political aspects. | Polarization (Social
sciences)—Political aspects. | Social media—Political aspects. | Internet—Political
aspects. | Identity politics. | Political culture.
Classification: LCC HM851 .L96 2019 | DDC 302.23/1—dc23
LC record available at https://lccn.loc.gov/2019014604

ISBN 978-1-63149-791-9 pbk.

Liveright Publishing Corporation, 500 Fifth Avenue, New York, N.Y. 10110
www.wwnorton.com

W. W. Norton & Company Ltd., 15 Carlisle Street, London W1D 3BS

1 2 3 4 5 6 7 8 9 0

To Terry, who keeps me humble, or tries to

The concept of "truth" as something dependent upon facts largely outside human control has been one of the ways in which philosophy hitherto has inculcated the necessary element of humility. When this check upon pride is removed, a further step is taken on the road towards a certain kind of madness—the intoxication of power which invaded philosophy with Fichte, and to which modern men, whether philosophers or not, are prone. I am persuaded that this intoxication is the greatest danger of our time, and that any philosophy which, however unintentionally, contributes to it is increasing the danger of vast social disaster.

—BERTRAND RUSSELL

Who needs Google? My father already knows everything.

—INSCRIPTION ON A MUG

Contents

PREAMBLE: NO ORDINARY QUESTION 1

1. MONTAIGNE'S WARNING 9

    Nothing More Wretched 9

    Like Ears of Corn 14

    A Very Social Attitude 18

2. THE OUTRAGE FACTORY 27

    Google Knows All 27

    Fake News and Information Pollution 30

    Sharing Emotions 35

3. WHERE THE SPADE TURNS 51

    Why We Don't Change Our Minds 51

    What Kind of Person Are You? 53

    From Belief to Conviction 62

4. IDEOLOGIES OF ARROGANCE
   AND THE AMERICAN RIGHT   75

   Roots of Authoritarianism.   75

   Telling It Like It Is   79

   The Logic of Status Threat   84

   Arrogance, Ignorance, and Contempt   92

5. LIBERALISM AND THE PHILOSOPHY
   OF IDENTITY POLITICS   103

   Arrogant Liberals   103

   Misunderstanding the Politics of Identity   104

   The Rationality Brand   121

   The Politics of Contempt   130

6. TRUTH AND HUMILITY AS DEMOCRATIC VALUES. .   139

   Socratic Lessons   139

   Intellectual Humility   149

   A Space of Reasons   154

   Truth and Democracy   163

ACKNOWLEDGMENTS   171

NOTES   173

REFERENCES AND ADDITIONAL SOURCES   183

INDEX   197

KNOW-IT-ALL SOCIETY

Preamble: No Ordinary Question

THE problem of politics is no ordinary question, Socrates says in *The Republic*; it concerns how we ought to live.[1] This book is about a particular version of the Socratic question: how we ought to *believe*. Or to put it more precisely, it concerns how we should go about the business of acquiring and maintaining our political convictions.

It is a pressing question. One reason it is pressing is that we are living in a time when not just political norms but the norms of evidence themselves are unsettled. There is increasingly very little common ground between the narratives of the Left and the Right, even the most trivial details of fact are disputed and questioned, and "fake news" has simply become a label for news that one doesn't like. In such times, the question of how to go about figuring out what to think is very much a living existential question.

Or it should be. But in fact, the unsettledness of our norms is making us not more reflective, but less. Judging by the tenor of our political discourse, our answer to the question of how we should believe seems to be: *as dogmatically as possible*. Recent data suggests that people from different sides of the political spectrum, at least in the United States, still agree more than they disagree on many issues. But this same data also shows that, increasingly, we regard the other party with suspicion—as dishonest, uninformed, and downright immoral.[2] The idea that we should listen to their views seems unthinkable. Moreover, we know the other side regards us the same way, and *we resent them for it*. The Right sees liberals as arrogant know-it-alls, while the Left retorts that this is precisely the description of the person the conservatives elected president of the United States.

But maybe both sides have a point. Maybe all of us, in a certain sense, are know-it-alls, and that's part of the problem.

America, as a culture, has never lacked confidence. We like to think of ourselves as A number one, top of the list, king of the hill—and deserving special attention because that is so. And self-esteem, cultural or otherwise, is mainly a very good thing. But if there is a single attitude most closely associated with our national consciousness at this political moment, it's not confidence. It's arrogance. In particular, a certain *kind* of arrogance that now defines our political relationships with each other. It's the arrogance of moral certainty—of thinking your side has it all figured out, that you don't need to improve because you are just so great already. It is arrogance about what we believe or think we know—intellectual arrogance.

Several factors are conspiring to encourage the spread of this attitude. The most obvious is our politics. In the United States, in particular, we are becoming numb not only to outrageous falsehoods, but to the bizarre self-assurance with which they are pronounced. We were told crowds were bigger than they were, that the sun shone when it didn't, that Trump won in a landslide—and that was just in the first few days after his election. Since then, our political discourse has become even more polluted with arrogant indifference to truth. Most of us have probably felt at some point or other that it can't get worse—and then it does.

All this highlights another reason our Socratic question is pressing. It is pressing because *how* we go about believing has a direct effect on what we believe. If we approach the question of whether to believe that climate change is real, or that vaccines cause autism, with our minds already made up, we will get an answer that reflects ourselves more than the truth. But more than that, if we become convinced that those who answer differently are also approaching the question with minds made up, we may begin to feel that the whole enterprise is bankrupt. We may begin to listen to those who tell us that everyone is entitled to their alternative facts, that all news is fake news and social media simply weaponized information. We may begin to think, with Camus, that "dialogue and personal relations have been replaced by propaganda or polemic."[3] In other words, the dogmatic arrogance we see in our political discourse may be due to our belief in our tribe's infallibility, or it may be due to the fact that we've simply punted on truth and embraced power as the measure of our success.

These reflections suggest that our Socratic question is really about our attitudes toward truth, both in life and in politics. How we should approach truth in politics is a problem with a long history. The current political situation with the presidency in the United States, or the recent presidential election in Brazil, or nationalist movements in Hungary, Austria, and even Great Britain, only serve to bring it into bold relief. The resolution of those situations, whatever that may turn out to be in each case, will not make the underlying problem go away. The more we come to think that tribal convictions are all that should matter, the more we arrogantly dismiss evidence for victory and truth for power, the weaker our grip on democracy becomes, no matter who is in power. Children raised in such an environment will absorb the lessons it gives them: that language is best used for hypocrisy and confusion, and democracy is for fools. As Arendt put it, "The result of a consistent and total substitution of lies for factual truth is not that the lies will now be accepted as truth, and the truth be defamed as lies, but that the sense by which we take our bearings in the real world . . . is being destroyed."[4]

It is tempting to think that these problems can be handled with technical, policy-driven solutions: reimagining our digital platforms, or passing new legislation, or teaching people more facts about civics. And without a doubt, those things are terribly important. But at the end of the day, dealing with our attitudes toward truth and conviction won't be solved just by teaching people more facts when we don't agree on what counts as a "fact." The problem of how to deal with the spread of dogmatism and the politics of arrogance is not a technical problem; it is a human problem. If we want to solve it, we have to change how and what we value; we must change our attitudes.

An attitude is an explicit or implicit mental evaluation that we make of the world around us; it is a frame of mind, a kind of positive or negative mental orientation. Attitudes have been much discussed in social psychology for over a century, and in philosophy long before that; the seventeenth- and eighteenth-century Scottish philosopher David Hume might have called them sentiments. And scientists since Freud have warned us that the mental attitudes driving us are often ones we would consciously disavow and be embarrassed to find ourselves holding. Our attitudes matter for how we relate to the world, to one another, and to ourselves.

You might think the idea that really matters in our polarized political landscape is civility. But while I have nothing against civility (except when "be civil" is used as code for "shut up"), I am concerned with something more fundamental. Civility marks a social norm, a baseline of appropriate social conduct. But how we *act* is the result of how we *think*—what we believe and therefore think we know. So if we want to understand our "uncivil" behavior, we must start with our attitudes toward our beliefs. Belief informs action—both within and without politics. Whether we cooperate or interfere with someone, whether we enact a policy or protest against it, who we vote for and why—all depend on what we believe. And it is important to understand not only those beliefs themselves, but our attitudes toward how we form them, how reliable they are, and how willing we are to change them.

We need to come to grips with how we regard both ourselves and others as believers.

It is for this reason that intellectual arrogance is such a useful focus for understanding the challenges facing democracy. Unlike incivility, intellectual arrogance is essentially concerned with beliefs—both our own and others'. When we suffer from it, we think we have nothing to learn from anyone else—that our worldview can't improve from hearing what people with different perspectives have to say.

But intellectual arrogance is not just an individual failing. I hope to convince you that it is also a social failing. In the right conditions, arrogance can go *tribal* and become an attitude that "we" have toward "them." And when that happens, we have started down the road toward an undemocratic future, since what I will call "tribal arrogance" causes us to put loyalty before truth and believe not only in the superiority of our views but—much more dangerously—in the superiority of our humanity.

The root of the problem is a tendency for conviction to give rise to arrogance. Thus my account rests on several, typically unnoticed, facts about the role that conviction plays in our lives. A conviction is a belief that takes on the mantle of commitment— a call to action—because it reflects our self-identity. It reflects the kind of person we aspire to be, and the kinds of groups and tribes we wish to belong to. That is why attacks on our convictions seem like attacks on our identity—because they are. But that is also why we often ignore evidence against our convictions; to give them up would be to change who we imagine ourselves to be.

That is a fact about the human condition. Its unnoticed consequence is that in unsettled times, humans are apt to go about the business of forming their political convictions in a very defensive, identity-protective way. But it also means we are ripe, during such times, for being taken advantage of. It is entirely human to want to be confident in your convictions, to be confident in yourself and your tribe.[5] But that desire for confidence, coupled with a fear of change, makes people vulnerable to political ideologies that would exploit these facts for authoritarian ends. Ideologies of arrogance, on both the Left and the Right, exploit our fears and desires by selling us cultural narratives not just of "us and them" but of "us *over* them." And these same ideologies encourage us to expand our identities by expanding our convictions, by giving everything around us a political meaning, and therefore making our every choice—from the clothes we wear, to the cars we drive, to the coffee we drink—a matter of conviction.

It also tends to go unnoticed that currently, we are doing all of this to ourselves. To understand how these cultural narratives develop, you have to understand where we communicate them: on the digital landscape. Information pollution—fake news and propaganda—accelerates the spread of group polarization and the sense that "we" know and "they" don't. They are effective not mainly because they get people to believe false things. They are effective because they get people to feel certain things, to share attitudes that reinforce their convictions and thus their identity. Social media, I'll argue, is a blind-conviction machine.

This book may seem like the literary equivalent of waving

your hands and pointing at where the real problem lies—even while everyone else, not caring about the causes of the fire, heads for the exit. But it also hopes to plant the seeds for an alternative ideal—one that sees conviction as no enemy of reason and evidence. Bertrand Russell once began a book defending the importance of rational argument in politics by admitting that "if such an opinion became common it would completely transform our social life and our political system." But, he added, dryly, "since both are at present faultless, this must weigh against it."[6] Like Russell's defense of rationality, a plea for less arrogance and more intellectual humility is easy to dismiss as idealistic and unneeded. Unneeded because we are all prone to think that it is only the other guy who is arrogant, and everyone knows that already, so why bother? Idealistic because we all know that nothing ever changes.

I confess my idealism—but I do not apologize. It is in the nature of philosophy to aspire to ideals, and to try to learn from our failing to meet them. It is these goals that this book aims to meet by diagnosing our culture's current obsession with self-certainty and abstracting from that a political lesson about the value of truth in democracy. In the end, the essence of that lesson is already contained in Socrates's query. To live is to have conviction, to tie your beliefs to action. We cannot take seriously the question of how to live without also taking seriously the question of how to believe.

I

Montaigne's Warning

Nothing More Wretched

Who hasn't thought—after an angry election, or an especially rancorous holiday meal with relatives, or simply in response to the numbing hostilities of the twenty-four-hour news cycle—of simply walking away from politics? Of just curling up with a good book and checking out of the world? For many people today, that probably just means getting off social media. For Michel de Montaigne, a minor nobleman, politician, and eventually one of the greatest writers of the sixteenth century, it meant something far more literal. At the age of thirty-eight, he retired to a tower, stocked it with books, and tried to drop out of political life.

Politics had left Montaigne in a skeptical frame of mind. Humanity likes to think of itself on a busy quest for truth, he thought, "but is it within the capacity of Man to find what he is looking for?" Montaigne was doubtful. There was a "plague" on Man: "the opinion that he knows something."[1]

The France of Montaigne's day was going through a period of extremely violent political and intellectual upheaval. The scientific discoveries of Copernicus had shaken the educated European's worldview, which took Earth as the center of the universe; the discovery of the New World threw into doubt the centrality of Europe itself. Most dramatically for the average person, the Catholic Church's traditional claim to be the sole arbiter of truth was under assault by the Protestant Reformation.

These three storms of doubt—about the nature of the universe, geography, and religious knowledge—left people feeling unsettled. Prophecies of doom were rampant; the apocalypse, or at least the end of civilization, was thought to be nigh. But most people did not react to these challenges to their belief systems by questioning whether they had things right. Far from it; religious extremism was rampant, with each group convinced that its side alone had discovered the religious truths of the universe. The uncertainty of the times justified in many people's minds drastic action and a ferocious, blind faith. As a result, cities and towns throughout France—including in Montaigne's own region—witnessed citizens of one religious persuasion slaughtering neighbors who were of a different persuasion. Those who advocated moderation or suggested that the solution to the religious wars was really political, not spiritual, were regarded with suspicion by both sides. Massive uncertainty over belief had fueled not diffidence but dogmatism.

Born in 1533, Montaigne spent his life navigating these conflicts, serving as mayor of Bordeaux, and surviving civil wars, various personal attacks, and the religious hostilities that had littered France with corpses.[2] Although he later reentered political life, Montaigne was not impressed by the rampant dogmatism of his day, saying at one point, "Zeal works wonders when it strengthens our tendency toward hatred . . . [but it] never makes one go flying towards goodness."[3] He preferred, he said, to retreat into his tower and into "the arms of learned virgins." It was there he wrote his famous essays, a form of writing he invented. They sparkle with observations about humanity but especially about himself, including his own tendency to fall victim to the same plague of vanity and arrogance that he saw in others.

In this endeavor he was inspired by the example of Socrates, who had advised, eighteen hundred years before Montaigne, that the path to wisdom begins with knowing yourself. The Oracle of Delphi had pronounced that no one was wiser than Socrates, but Socrates himself said he knew only that he didn't know much. Montaigne's writings are sprinkled with references to the ancient Greek philosopher, whose constant searching for answers he admired. But Montaigne's real obsession was with a subtly different group of thinkers—the ancient Pyrrhonian skeptics, who maintained that what made people unhappy was their tendency to think they knew more than they actually did. Unlike Socrates, however, the Pyrrhonians didn't encourage people to know more. If we want to be happy, they said, we should just give up on the quest for knowledge. Indeed, we should even give up on believing anything at all.

The resolutely Catholic Montaigne hesitated to go that far. It wasn't faith per se that was the problem, he thought, but our penchant for intellectual arrogance—*arrogance about our beliefs or our worldview.* This is what he took from the skeptics, and he inscribed their sayings into the beams of his library, including this remark from Pliny: "There is nothing certain except that nothing is certain, and nothing more wretched than Man nor more arrogant."[4] "Arrogant" was Montaigne's watchword, and his warning: our desire for certainty, for thinking that we've figured everything out, that our reasons are the best reasons, is what gets us into trouble, both in politics and in life.

This book is written in light of Montaigne's warnings about the dangers of intellectual arrogance. Like Montaigne, we are living in an age of severe disruption. For some Americans, much of that disruption concerns a changing economic, cultural, and demographic landscape—one in which white Americans will soon no longer be in the majority. But part of the disruption is technological. Information technology has changed how we live, how we learn about the world, and how we interact with one another. It has made it easier to access information than ever before, yet we increasingly seem to disagree over that information, over what we know.

We are increasingly polarized in our attitudes toward our political opponents. And we disagree now not only over values, and not only over facts, but over which sources for those facts are even reliable. Our public discourse has been trampled as a result. Traditional boundaries and norms of civility have been set aside, and almost nothing seems to surprise any of us anymore. But how do we react to this uncertainty? Like the religious zealots of the sixteenth century, we generally don't doubt; we dig in. We tell ourselves that we know what is right and what is wrong, reassuring ourselves with every tweet about our own superiority.

By the time Montaigne retreated to his tower, the dogmatism of his age had already done its bloody work. We are not there yet, but dogmatic politics based on a sense of superiority, on a perceived grasp of the real truth, is on the rise again. We see it in the marches of neo-Nazis on college campuses, in the demonstrations in Europe, in the desire to build a wall along our nation's borders, in the dismissal of compromise by both the Right and the Left. It is hard to shake the feeling that our path is leading us into a dark wood—a path lit by the shining intensity of dogma, self-certainty, and intellectual arrogance.

Montaigne's own reaction to the widespread intellectual arrogance of his day vividly illustrates the philosophical problem we'll grapple with throughout this book. It is a problem that preceded him and will remain after us. It is a single problem with two faces—one personal and one political. The personal face concerns what sort of attitude we should adopt toward our own convictions—about what we think is fundamentally right and what is wrong. Put in the form of a question to oneself, it amounts to this: How can I be open to the possibility of being wrong while still maintaining strong conviction? The one attitude seems to psychologically rule out the other. This is a problem for any reflective person, and as Montaigne would have been the first to attest, it is no mere abstract puzzle but an existential issue, for it concerns how to live and how to think. It concerns how to retain conviction without intellectual arrogance.

Not believing anything is not really an option, as Montaigne knew, but retreating to a tower is not really an option for most of us either, and neither is it all that helpful from the standpoint of social change. And that brings us to the political face of the problem. It was doubtless felt in Montaigne's time, but for democracies it takes a particularly acute form. Democracies need their citizens to have convictions, for an apathetic electorate is no electorate at all. Yet democracies also need their citizens to listen to one another's convictions, to engage in political give-and-take. The problem is that those with conviction regard with suspicion those listening to the other side; they aren't true believers. And those who listen often *do* fall into inaction; they flee to the tower, ivory or otherwise.

The problem that intellectual arrogance causes for politics is not unique to us, but as in Montaigne's time, it is particularly pressing. In order to grapple with it, we must first understand what it is.

Like Ears of Corn

The seeds of arrogance are planted early in life. The best we can hope for, Montaigne thought, is to be like ears of corn—which stand proud and erect when their heads are young and empty, but droop with humility when their heads are old and full.[5] But in reality, he argued, that never really happens. For Montaigne and the ancient skeptics, our tendency to overestimate our knowledge isn't just a phase; it is part of human nature.

In recent decades, cognitive science has been catching up to Montaigne. The psychologist David Dunning and his colleagues, for example, asked subjects to first perform tasks like checking sentences for bad grammar, and then rate themselves on how well they performed that task.[6] Those who did poorly tended to think they performed better than they did, while those who did better tended to think they performed worse. These results have been replicated numerous times, with students, in various job settings, even with doctors. One lesson is that the competent not only have skill but they know what it means to have that skill. Those who know tend to be harder on themselves—because they know how easy it is to make a mistake. But the incompetent don't know what they don't know, so they are more prone to overconfidence.

Moreover, most of us think we know more about how the world around us works than we really do. One of the most famous results in cognitive science is the "illusion of explanatory depth": When asked first to rate how well they understand how a zipper works and then to explain it, almost everyone thinks they know, but they really don't.[7] And that finding, too, is highly replicated: we think we understand all sorts of things better than we do.[8] Given that none of us are experts about everything, it is hard to avoid the conclusion that we all remain a bit of a teenager at heart: we stand tall like young corn only because our heads are empty.

Our tendency to overrate our knowledge is related to our more general tendency to think that our judgments are more rational and deliberate then they really are. As Montaigne suggested half a millennium ago, our "rational souls accept notions and opinions" produced during "waking sleep"—that is, produced without the aid of conscious reflection.[9]

Seventeenth- and eighteenth-century philosophers following Montaigne developed this insight. They divided the mind into different systems, or "faculties": those that operated automatically, or passively; and those that were more conscious, active, and deliberate.[10] "Intuition" is our capacity to make unreflective, automatic judgments; "reflection" is our capacity to engage in complex problem solving, plan for the long term, and consciously weigh reasons. While reflection is what enables us to engage in more sophisticated cognitive activities, intuition is indispensable right from the get-go. We could not get on with our lives if our minds did not quickly process the vast majority of information that regularly confronts us—if the mind did not take intuitive shortcuts.[11]

One example is our tendency to automatically and unconsciously compare and contrast new things and experiences with those already familiar to us.[12] This is why we often find ourselves liking situations, clothing, food, and so on that are similar to what we already know. But it is also why we quickly try to make things cohere with what we've come to expect. Ask someone, for example, how many animals Moses took with him on his ark, and they may not spot the error—simply because they are unconsciously associating Noah with arks. This kind of process is one element of what David Hume—an eighteenth-century Scottish philosopher deeply influenced by Montaigne—described as the "association of ideas," and what he thought was one of the mechanisms most used by the mind. As Hume suggested, such associative thinking spares us the trouble of consciously and individually evaluating each new object we encounter, and it means that we can make judgments faster and with "more method and regularity."[13] But it also means that our opinions, and even how we perceive the world, are *shaped* by what we already believe and feel to be true—whether or not it really is true.[14] We stain the world with our sentiments, as Hume famously put it.

This is the heart of the phenomena now called "motivated reasoning" and "implicit bias." To some degree we see what we *expect* to see and believe what fits with what we already think we know. And the more familiar we are with certain categories—including what to associate with, and expect from, members of those categories—the more automatic and involuntary our judgments concerning those categories become.[15]

All this means we can also get things very wrong, and in morally troubling ways, for this tendency to intuitively associate new with old is not limited to inanimate objects but includes people as well.[16] And it is shot through with social norms and prejudice. Which, in turn, means that racist, sexist, or otherwise discriminatory associations that have permeated the larger social context can distort our perceptions of one another. The pervasive stereotype that Muslims are dangerous can distort the ways in which we come to think of, and treat, Muslim people; the pervasive stereotype that women are less self-assured or intelligent than men can distort the ways in which we come to think of, and treat, women;

the pervasive stereotype that black people are dangerous distorts the ways in which we think of, and treat, black people; and so on.[17] And, the more pervasive the stereotypes are, the more likely they are to influence how people conceive of certain groups, and the more inclined those people will be to assume they "know" what individuals in those groups really are like.[18]

To make matters even worse, we are also really bad at telling the difference between beliefs formed on the basis of reflection and those formed on the basis of implicit bias. In staining the world with our sentiments, we are prone to bias blind spots: we fail to recognize when our *own* judgments are informed by biases. Other folks are biased, sure. But *our* beliefs (we tell ourselves) are pure as the driven snow, based on facts and sound reasoning.[19] Combine that faulty perception with the finding, stated earlier, that we overestimate how good we are at tasks that we are really bad at—and you get the frightening possibility that *the worse we are at detecting our biases, the better we think we are.*

Montaigne and Hume would not be surprised.

A Very Social Attitude

It is difficult not to feel for Icarus. He tried to fly like the gods, but he fell to earth, burning out rather than fading away. In so doing, he paid the price of what the Greeks called hubris. Judging by their myths, they were a bit obsessed with it. In their stories, hubris never escapes punishment. Niobe, who boasted of the superiority of her children, was turned to stone; Prometheus, who stole fire from the gods, had his liver eaten for eternity; Icarus, who flew too close to the sun, dropped into the sea.

But while you can read these myths as cautionary tales, you can also see in them a recognition of a very human truth: that overconfidence is a central feature of life. It is risky, as the Greeks emphasized, but, as their fables also suggest, we tend to think that nothing great is achieved without it. "Fortune commonly favors the bold and enterprising," David Hume noted, "and nothing inspires us with more boldness than a good opinion of ourselves."[20] Self-esteem, said Hume, is an essential part of any successful character and habit of mind.

In our own time, we've come to absorb this truism as liberating. Starting in the 1970s, the self-esteem movement in education was a reaction to an earlier culture that hammered at students' self-conception and derided those who were in any way different, creative, or outside the white, heterosexual mainstream. The new approach emphasized praise and achievement rather than criticism. More recently, there has been a similar fascination with the related concept of "grit." Grit is a drive to succeed. It is a kind of determination and, as such, is often marked by self-control. The person with grit is the person who sticks it out; it's the kid who doesn't eat the marshmallow. Grit is what pushes us through, keeps us at it when the odds are against us. And having grit, we tend to assume, means having self-esteem.

Importantly, we also apply Hume's truism to our beliefs. We

admire the woman whose self-esteem enables her to stand and testify about her experience of sexual assault even as those arrayed against her try to undermine her credibility. And we admire Galileo, who confidently believed that evidence showed that the Earth traveled around the sun, even though this view was dismissed by both the church and other scientists of his day. We admire, in short, those who have the strength of mind to go with the evidence even when few others find it plausible, much less believe it.

And we should. Self-confidence, either about our abilities or our beliefs, is a very good thing; we hope to instill it in our children, and we wish we had more of it ourselves. We demand it from those who fly our planes, operate on our bodies, and lead our armies in battle, and we reward it with esteem, with medals, with power. Confidence is sexy; no one follows the fainthearted or the meek. And while we realize that confidence can become overconfidence, and boldness hubris, we are often willing to bet on those confident enough to take risks, as long as they are more often right than wrong. Confidence, in short, is socially rewarding.

The undeniable social and psychological benefits of confidence help to explain why human beings are prone to overconfidence as well as intellectual arrogance. The explanation lies not with confidence per se but with *our socially reinforced desire for confidence*. We long for the esteem of others, and having self-esteem is an excellent way to get it. That's true about our beliefs too. We want other people to agree with us, to flatter our opinions with praise, and being confident in your opinions can often help achieve that end.

A similar point is true of our tendency to inflate our knowledge. We saw earlier that this tendency is partly the result of our hardwired propensity for quick, intuitive associative thinking and our willingness to overlook our own biases. But it is not our ignorance alone that matters as much as our *fear of ignorance*. While we don't know the extent of what we don't know, and we often overestimate how much we do know, we are all too familiar with what it is like to get things wrong or not know the answer. Nobody wants that. And for good reason: mistakes can get you hurt. They aren't socially rewarded either. You don't win awards for making mistakes, and you don't get promoted for admitting how much you don't know. So we try to signal to others—and importantly, to ourselves—that we are reliable and knowledgeable. That's what makes the human condition so deliciously ironic. We so strongly hate not knowing that we try to convince ourselves—and everyone else—we know more than we do.

What all this suggests is that seeds of intellectual arrogance are planted in the soil of our social interactions. One seed is not ignorance itself but our socially reinforced fear of it; the other is not confidence itself but our socially reinforced desire to have it. Combine this fear and desire and you get a social recipe for encouraging people to resist admitting error and act as if they are always right, even when they are wrong.

Intellectual arrogance is therefore a very social attitude—both in its origins, as we've just seen, and also simply in itself. The know-it-all's defining characteristic is, in fact, explicitly social: he thinks he has nothing to learn from anyone else—that his worldview can't improve from hearing what people with a different perspective have to say. Naturally, experts often don't need anyone's help to do what they know best. (A pilot isn't arrogant just because she doesn't take tips on how to land the airplane from someone who doesn't know the first thing about flying.) But as we've seen, those who know the most often tend to recognize that they don't know it all. And experts sometimes seek out additional training and coaching. They know you have to work hard to up your game—whether the game is sports or science.

A telling example of this point crops up in Thomas Ricks's 2006 book, *Fiasco*, about the beginning of the Iraq War. Ricks details how many senior military officers were alarmed by the administration's absurdly optimistic projections of how much the war would cost, how difficult it would be to maintain control over conquered Iraqi territory, and how many American troops it would take to do so effectively. Ricks reports one four-star general as telling him that these concerns were "blown off" and "discounted" by senior White House officials, even before they got to the president:

"The people around the president were so, frankly, intellectually arrogant," this general continued. "They *knew* that postwar Iraq would be easy and would be a catalyst for change in the Middle East. They were making simplistic assumptions and refused to put them to the test . . . they did it because they already had the answers and they wouldn't subject their hypothesis to examination. These were educated men, they are smart men. But they are not wise men."[21]

This passage illustrates one of the defining features of intellectual arrogance: an unwillingness to regard your own worldview as capable of improvement from the evidence and the experience of others. But it also suggests a second important characteristic of the intellectually arrogant: they put ego before truth—but tell themselves they are doing the opposite. The intellectually arrogant are convinced their views are superior because of their better command of the facts. But in reality, their sense of superiority reflects their own hyperconcern for their self-esteem.[22] Their posture is defensive; fear of error and desire for esteem push them to emphasize their authority, and thus to insist on their being right, whether they are or not. That defensive posture not only can keep them from seeing the evidence; it makes them believe their own hype.

Examples abound—from the "smartest guys in the room" at Enron to the "best and brightest" in the Kennedy and Johnson administrations who got America embroiled in Vietnam. Intellectual arrogance blinds us to mistakes. This is the heart of the somewhat misleading proverb "Pride goeth before a fall"—which is deceiving because justified pride is no more dangerous than justified confidence. But intellectual arrogance *can* be dangerous, precisely because it involves a confusion of ego with truth. When you see yourself as one of the "smartest guys in the room," you see yourself as confident and strong, and you think your view must be right because, well, it is yours. But that confidence just makes you miss obvious facts, precisely because you think you know all the facts already.

The delusional nature of intellectual arrogance explains why people rarely see it in themselves. But we can spot it in others. There's the paradigmatic drunk uncle who weighs in on any political topic and always sees his own opinion as the last word. This is the guy no one wants to sit next to at Thanksgiving, who smugly tells those whose experience he knows little about what they should be feeling and thinking, who refuses to acknowledge alternative viewpoints as anything other than fake news. Then there is the person who, while civil and seemingly reflective, never changes her view or even admits that she might need to think about things from a different perspective. Over time you realize she is not actively listening to what you say, but only waiting for her turn to speak. There is the ubiquitous man who refuses to accept other people's points except when he repackages them as his own personal insight. Someone like this might *seem* open to new ideas; he listens, maybe even learns, but he doesn't see himself as learning from *others*. He sees his beliefs as being improved by his own genius.[23] The fact that we recognize these characters so easily is a sign of the pervasiveness of intellectual arrogance.

Like other socially oriented attitudes, intellectual arrogance is interpersonal and dependent on context. People can be intellectually arrogant on certain topics but receptive and humble about their knowledge of others. But intellectual arrogance is also typically directed at particular kinds of people or sources of information. Someone who is intellectually arrogant feels superior, and typically, people feel superior not just in general but toward a person or a kind of person in particular. And that is what makes intellectual arrogance politically important and troublesome: it can become tribal.

Attitudes are often contagious; any group can rapidly come to share almost any attitude. When we feel happy, or sad, or fearful, others around us can come to those same feelings. An attitude becomes tribal, however, when it is not just shared by a group but is implicitly or unconsciously *social in its content—that is, experienced as part of a "we" and directed at a "them."* Racist attitudes are a prime example, as are attitudes of contempt or resentment when we direct them at entire groups of people. Intellectual arrogance, too, is most virulent when it is tribal. Tribal (intellectual) arrogance means being arrogant toward *others* because they are not like us: they are Republicans or Democrats, African Americans or immigrants, atheists or religious believers. *We know*; "they" don't. We have nothing to learn from them, and our capacities for knowing (or knowing about a specific topic) are superior, more developed, more refined.

Tribal arrogance is therefore *intrinsically hierarchical*. It is the arrogance of whites over nonwhites, of men over women, of native-born over immigrant. But it is also the arrogance of the educated over the uneducated, the rich over the poor, the cosmopolitan over the provincial. For the tribally arrogant, those in other tribes are like children, and for that reason, there is a sad history of the arrogant denying rights to those they consider inferior, precisely because they view those "inferior" people as having less of a capacity to reason and to know.

When we become tribally arrogant toward others, we go beyond experiencing arrogance as a mere attitude. Attitudes can come and go: one can be arrogant on Tuesday but not on Wednesday. But tribal arrogance is typically more of a mind-set, by which I mean a collection of attitudes and beliefs about your tribal convictions and knowledge and their superiority over others. Mind-sets are less transitory. They become fixed and rigid, and hard to shake. That's why tribal arrogance, when pervasive, is so very dangerous.

While he didn't speak about it in the same terms, this danger was something Montaigne knew all too well. Our arrogant assurance in the superiority of what he called our own habits and customs could lead to the worst in humanity. "I live in a season when unbelievable examples of this vice of cruelty flourish because of the license of our civil wars; you can find nothing in ancient history more extreme than what we witness every day."[24] This is Montaigne's warning about intellectual arrogance: once it becomes tribal, it dehumanizes and destroys. That's a warning as relevant today as it was almost five centuries ago. To heed it, we must understand not only the social conditions that give rise to this attitude but the factors promoting its spread in our culture right now.

2

❖

The Outrage Factory

Google Knows All

Much of what we know we "Google-know." The internet is our go-to source of information on almost any topic. It is what we check first—and what we check last, using it to settle our disputes both banal and profound. How many times has someone you know pronounced on some point of fact and everyone else in the room races to their phones to verify or falsify it? We routinely use googling to trump other forms of inquiry, even to question experts. While we all know that googling can lead us astray, that doesn't stop us from using it routinely, or from regarding it as essentially reliable on a broad range of topics. Indeed, for most of us, searching online happens without much forethought. It is just the obvious, immediate first step in answering almost any question about the social world; for those questions, it has a kind of priority.[1] We trust it.

Our reliance on Google-knowing turns out to feed our natural tendency to overinflate what we know. The devices we carry around in our pockets give us access to a world of information at the tip of our fingers (or thumbs). No wonder we feel more knowledgeable with our phones in our hands, as the psychologist Matthew Fisher found in studying the relationship between internet searches and the illusion of explanatory depth. In his study, Fisher again asked different groups questions, like "How does a zipper work?"[2] The first group was encouraged to search the internet to check on their explanations; a second group was not allowed to use outside sources. Then each group was asked to rate how much they knew about topics that had *nothing to do with* the first question they had been asked (in this case, nothing to do with the way zippers work). The result? Those who had searched the internet rated their ability to know answers to unrelated questions higher than those who had not been allowed to search the internet. Merely searching the internet convinces people that they know more than they do—even about things they haven't yet researched. It is as if the sheer speed and ease of access to information on the internet causes us to lose track of how much we rely on it, thereby "distorting how we view our own abilities."[3] And that makes us think we know more than we do. Of course we're right, we think—just google it!

Yet the most important fact about Google-knowing—and indeed about our entire online life over the last decade—is not how much information it gives us, but the fact that *it gives us just the information we want.* The Internet of Things is really an Internet of Us, our fingers busily curating our online lives, visiting the sites we want, using the apps we want, and carefully crafting our Facebook experience so it reflects the image we want. Our online life, in other words, is deeply personalized. That's because Facebook, Google, and most of our apps, search engines, and social platforms all work in the same basic way, different algorithms aside. They attempt to track people's preferences by way of tracking their likes, their clicks, their searches, or their friends. That data is then analyzed and used to predict what a given person's current and future preferences will be. It is used to predict what sort of information you—and crucially, those similar to you—will find interesting, what posts you will like, and what links you will click. This preference aggregation then helps to dictate the results of your searches, and what you see on the various platforms you use. That is why those shoes you were thinking of buying are being advertised on your Facebook feed. And these same algorithms help predict not only what we'll click and like next but what we'll buy, who we'll find attractive, and how we'll vote. As a result, both our online *and* offline lives are increasingly tailored—meant to satisfy our preexisting preferences.

It seems likely, even obvious, that the preference-tracking structure of our digital platforms is playing a part in our growing know-it-all-ism. That's not because the internet has any dark power all its own. It just feeds into our human tendency to over-inflate what we know by reinforcing what we already believe.

Googling is like being in a room with a million shouting voices. It is only natural that many of us hear the voices most similar to our own, shouting what we already believe; as a result, Google can find you confirmation for almost anything, no matter how weird. No wonder there has been an explosion of dogmatism. The mechanisms that make Google-knowing possible make us not only individually overconfident about what we understand but overconfident about what our tribe understands. The internet becomes one big reinforcement mechanism, obtaining for each one of us the information that we are already biased to believe, and encouraging us to regard those in other bubbles as misinformed miscreants.

But that doesn't just make us dogmatic and arrogant. It also makes us easy marks.

Fake News and Information Pollution

In December 2016, a man by the name of Edgar Welch entered a pizzeria in Washington, DC, armed with an assault rifle. Welch was there to "self-investigate" a bizarre conspiracy theory, according to which Hillary Clinton and other Democratic politicians were allegedly running a child sex-trafficking ring from the basement of the restaurant. To Welch's surprise, the theory turned out to be false. Not only was there no sex-trafficking ring in the basement; there wasn't even a basement. As Welch would later tell the *New York Times*, "The intel on this wasn't 100 percent."[4]

The dark fantasy that caused Welch to turn up in DC that day is the epitome of "fake news"—by which I mean deliberately misleading news stories that are spread for fun, profit, and political gain. And Welch's actions are widely cited as an example of the harm that fake news can do. Conspiracy stories like Pizzagate—and even weirder variants, like QAnon—are just one form of a broader phenomenon that we might call "information pollution." Information pollution is the dumping of potentially toxic information into the media environment. Information can be toxic in different ways, but the most obvious ways are by being false (misinformation), intentionally deceptive and misleading (disinformation), or simply not based on any evidence at all.

Information pollution is not new, nor are justifications of its use for political ends. Machiavelli advised that princes must always be ready to deceive, and to do so boldly. Benjamin Franklin apparently planted false stories about the Seneca Indians and their alliances with Britain for the purposes of swaying public opinion both in America and abroad. And *The Protocols of the Elders of Zion*, a virulent, made-up anti-Semitic text that is still in circulation today, was initially devised around 1905 for the purposes of stoking resistance to the Bolsheviks during the Russian Revolution.

Information has always been, and will continue to be, a chief tool of empire and war. It is by the use, and misuse, of information that those who desire to manipulate hearts and minds have always acted. And the purpose of that action is almost invariably the same: to rouse the passions of the ordinary citizen and to instill a dogmatic and unforgiving attitude. With this attitude instilled in them, people can be made to do the most inhuman things to each other. That is the case in totalitarian regimes, and it is the case in contemporary liberal democracies—where propaganda, while necessarily different in character, is no less effective.[5]

Yet while information pollution has been around as long as knives in the back, whispers in the ear, and the written word itself, we are living in a new golden age for information polluters. In large part, that is because of the preference-tracking nature of our digital platforms. Internet personalization is not just good for business; it is good for politics. Russian troll farms, political campaigns, and "research" firms (like the now despised Cambridge Analytica) use the personalized internet to help place targeted political advertisements and to get people to "like" and "follow" fake social-media accounts that feed them "news" reinforcing their political opinions. That's why the personalization of the internet is great when it comes to shopping for shoes, but terrible when it comes to shopping for facts. When the only facts you receive are those tailored to fit your biases, you are a ripe target for manipulation.[6]

Most people tend to assume that information pollution is wrong because it amounts to lying. But framing the issue solely in terms of lying actually underplays and mischaracterizes the danger. That danger isn't lies per se but deception. Lying is not quite the same thing as deception. To lie is to deliberately say what you believe to be false with the *intention* of deceiving your audience. I can deceive you without lying (silence at a key moment, for example, can be deceptive). And I can lie to you without deceiving—

either because you are skeptical and don't believe me, or because what I say is inadvertently true; either way, you are lied to but not deceived. You might be led to think that deception occurs when someone is actually caused to believe what is false. "Deception," as philosophers say, is a "success term." But that's only halfway there. Deception can happen even without false belief.

Reflect on that old con the shell game. The con man presents three shells, one of which has a coin underneath. He moves the shells around and asks you to pick the shell with the coin. If done right, it looks easy; but it isn't. Using sleight of hand, he distracts you so that you can't track the right shell and know where the penny is. But one can lack knowledge without having a false belief. One can be simply confused, and that is typically the case with such tricks. You don't know what to think, so you simply guess. You can be deceived not only by believing what is false but by *not* believing what is true.

The use of social media to spread political misinformation online is partly just a giant shell game. Propagandists often don't care whether everyone, or even most people, really believe the specific things they are selling. They don't have to get you to actually believe the penny is under the wrong shell. They just have to get you confused enough that you don't know what is true. That's still deception. And it is this kind of deception that dreadful for-profit conspiracy sites, and Russian-sponsored troll farms, have been particularly adept at spreading on social media. No doubt, some percentage of people actually believe such postings, but a far greater number of people come away ever so slightly more doubtful of what is true. They don't know what to believe.

It used to be that when someone would say something outrageously false (for example, "the moon landing was faked"), it would be ignored by most folks, who reasoned, "If that were true, I would have heard about it by now" (in other words, heard about it from creditable, independent sources). Filters (primarily, editors) worked not only to weed out the bad but to make sure the truly extraordinary real news came to the surface. The internet has made such reasoning moot, simply because so many of us are ensconced in our own information bubbles. Few people reject strange claims on the grounds that they haven't heard them before now, because chances are they already *have* heard them, or something close to them, from the sites that tend to confirm their biases.[7] That fact makes them more susceptible to accepting fake news, or at least not rejecting it. It makes them easier to confuse.

Even more insidiously, the tendency to accept bizarre claims actually can encourage us to be more close-minded and dogmatic—and for weirdly "rational" reasons. Part of being open-minded is taking relevant alternatives to your view seriously.[8] You look into the alternatives; if they check out, you modify your view. If they don't, you carry on. That, after all, is presumably what Edgar Welch tried to do. But as his case also illustrates, the internet has made many more alternatives relevant. And it has normalized crazy. Because for almost any view that you want to think is true—like, leading Democrats are selling children with pizza slices in DC—you can find "evidence" supporting it online. That means not only that some naïve people are deceived but also that the rest of us now need to decide which bizarre stories we pay attention to and which we dismiss. And because there is so much weirdness, we often dismiss stories out of hand when they don't emerge from sources we already trust. We don't really check out the alternatives, because (at least we tell ourselves) there are simply too many outrageous claims out there. And that's true, but the net result is that we are just spending more and more time reading news from sources geared to tell us exactly what we want to hear anyway.

That's got to be one of the saddest ironies in a time rich with them: the technology that allows us to know more than ever before can also turn us into close-minded dogmatists. And information pollution, while it feeds that fact, isn't the only reason. There's another, even more basic way that the internet encourages our know-it-all culture.

Sharing Emotions

One of David Hume's most famous philosophical maxims is that reason is the slave of the passions. His point is that while reason can tell us how to get someplace, it can't tell us where to go. Only the heart can tell us our ends; reason gives us the means. Hume himself was a man of large appetites, famous for his charisma, conversation, and literary ambition as much as his philosophy, which was ahead of its time and often shocking to his contemporaries. Another of his central insights was that human beings often deceive themselves about the role of passion in our lives. We know that emotions matter in love and war, but we fool ourselves into thinking they play a lesser role in our ordinary interactions with one another. Hume thought morality itself was based on our "social passions," and he felt that religion often misled us about the basis of moral distinctions. One doesn't have to agree with him on this to see the general point. Too often we think we are playing the game of reason when we are actually playing the game of passion. And Hume's point turns out to be crucial for understanding how our use of technology can unwittingly feed our tendency toward arrogance.

To see how, let's start by noting that, while useful, the term "information pollution" can be misleading. The metaphor assumes that the broader information culture that is being polluted, like nature, is already given and—save for the interventions of the polluters—pure. But it is we humans who make and convey information, and it is we who construct and live in the wider information culture. The internet is not just something that has happened to us; it is a world we've created. As every good propagandist knows, one can't seize hearts and minds without appealing to something that is already hidden deep within them. And so it is with fake news. We've created a digital world that reflects our tendency to care less about the truth than we profess, even while it encourages us to be more arrogant about our tribal convictions. In other words, we are living in not just a polluted information culture but a corrupted one.

Corruption is not the same as pollution. Pollution is something that happens to a system; corruption is something that happens *within* a system. One way social systems are corrupt is that sometimes their stated rules are not their real rules. A criminal justice system is corrupt, for example, if it purports to treat everyone fairly but actually discriminates on the basis of race, or when quid pro quo actions (such as favors on behalf of police or judges) are widespread. Likewise, an information culture is corrupt when the rules of evidence and reliability that some of its participants allegedly adhere to—their epistemic principles, in other words—are not the ones they more frequently employ.[9] This phenomenon might be what some people mean when they talk about living in a "post-truth" culture. Of course, we don't literally live in a world where nothing is true. Truth exists as much as it ever has. What has happened is that our information culture has become so corrupt as to tolerate and encourage self-deceptive attitudes toward truth and evidence. It encourages us to care more about our convictions than about truth, but to tell ourselves we are doing otherwise.

A small but telling example of how bad faith manifests itself online is the way some people reacted to the Pizzagate story. That story, recall, was very specific: Hillary Clinton was selling children for sex out of one particular pizza joint in Washington, DC. The story was widely circulated. By the time Mr. Welch pulled his Chuck Norris act, it had been running around various far-Right circles for months. Welch himself reported that he had heard it by word of mouth. He reportedly was surprised and "checked into it" by watching videos and reading stories on the internet. All of these stories claimed this was really happening: child abuse in a specific place.

So ask yourself: If you really believed this was happening, wouldn't you, too, try to do something? Well, some people did act—sort of. There were some scattered and very small protests—actually just a few folks standing across the street with signs. There were a lot of death threats—not just to those owning and working at the pizzeria, but apparently to those owning and working at business establishments up and down the block. Which is, frankly, bizarre, and no doubt frightening. But it is not a particularly effective way to stop a child-trafficking ring that was allegedly happening in a public establishment and that millions of people supposedly knew about. And in any event, death threats weren't the most common reaction. The most common reaction by those who claimed to believe this story was simply to pass it on, to repeat it, and to form other views based on it.

Even more interesting was the reaction within certain far-Right media circles following Mr. Welch's attack. It is a reaction that has become all too familiar. Immediately after the attack, the far Right began circulating the theory that Edgar Welch was a "crisis actor"; that is, he was paid by political interests on the Left to enter the pizzeria with a gun in order to embarrass far-Right conservatives.[10] These accusations—and similar charges about "false flag attacks"—are now ritualistically repeated following mass shootings in the United States. And they do not come out of the blue; civil rights protestors were often accused in the 1960s of being paid actors. So go conspiracy theories, you might say; there is no getting around their craziness. But this is a bit different: in the case of Edgar Welch, such accusations not only provided a weird spectacle but pointed to one way in which we corrupt our media environment. It was as if the Trump supporters who had insisted they believed the story now wanted to label *that very fact*—the fact they had believed it—"fake news." *They wanted to deny that anyone like them would act on a story that they constantly said required action.* This is bad faith and intellectual arrogance in action. And it shows how disinformation can corrupt as well as pollute.

It would be a grave mistake, however, to think that nutcase conspiracy theorists are the only ones corrupting our information culture. To some extent, we all do—at least those of us on social media. That's because, as I earlier noted, one way a system can be corrupted is by running on different rules than the "official" ones—the ones we think it runs on. This often happens on social media, which is designed to function as a vehicle for our passions more than for reason.

This fact manifests itself in ways we often don't realize—right down to the function of the communicative acts we engage in online. One of the things that many people—including many people reading this book—do on Facebook is post or share news stories. The posting of a news story can be seen as a communicative act. Our most common communicative acts are verbal, but written ones count too—memos, letters, and yes, Facebook and Twitter posts. Our communicative acts come in a variety of forms. We can question ("Is the door closed?") or command ("Close the door!")

or assert and describe ("The door is closed"). Sometimes—indeed, often—we are doing more than one thing at a time, such as when I say that the food at a particular restaurant is really tasty while we are wondering where to grab dinner. In that context, I could perform several communicative actions at once: assert that the food at that establishment is tasty, endorse the establishment as the place where we ought to eat, and just express my feelings of anticipation and hunger at the prospect of eating there.

When we share media stories online—especially when we do so without comment—we typically appear (to others and ourselves) to be doing something similar. We appear to be engaging in one or both of the following communicative acts: providing testimony—asserting that something is the case, typically assumed to be summed up by the headline (for example, "Hillary Clinton Suspected to Have Been Acting for Russians"); or endorsing or recommending a piece of information as worthy of attention or even belief, possibly even saying just that in a comment on the post ("Everyone should read this!").

That's not all we do with news stories that we post, naturally. Sometimes we aren't actually endorsing the story; we are sharing it as something we think is amusing, really dumb, or ironic. When we do something like that, the kind of act we are engaging in is self-consciously expressive; we are expressing our amusement, or ironic detachment, or frustration. We aren't trying to convey something factual. Yet although that happens, we don't assume it is the typical case—as evidenced by the fact that most people feel obligated to signal in some way that their act of sharing shouldn't be understood as endorsement. On Twitter, for example, it is not uncommon for people to declare on their profile page that "retweets are not endorsements." Such a declaration wouldn't make sense if the default assumption weren't that shares *are* endorsements.

So, shares typically *seem* to us like assertions and/or endorsements of assertions. But what if that appearance is just that: appearance and not reality? What if we are just confused about the way communication actually functions online? As it turns out, there are reasons to think that we are, in fact, confused.[11] These reasons concern both what we do and what we don't do when we share content online.

Let's start with what we don't do. Current research estimates that at least 60 percent of news stories shared online have not even been read by the person sharing them. In 2016, researchers at Columbia University, for example, arrived at this conclusion by cleverly studying the intersection between two data sets.[12] The first data set was made up of Twitter shares over the course of a month from five leading news sites—as tracked by tweets containing links to stories on those sites. The second set of data consisted of the clicks over the same period connected to that set of shortened links. The sets were massive—2.8 million shares responsible for seventy-five billion potential views, and almost ten million clicks. After designing a methodology for sorting through these correlations, and correcting for its biases, the researchers found that only four in ten people tweeting out news items have actually read them.[13] As one author of the study summed up the matter, "People are more willing to share an article than read it."[14]

So that's what we don't do: read what we are sharing. What we *do* is share content that gets people riled up. Research has found that the best predictor of sharing is strong *emotions*—both emotions like affection (think posts about cute kittens) and emotions like outrage. One study suggests that morally laden emotions are particularly effective: every moral sentiment in a tweet increases by 20 percent its chances of being shared.[15] And plausibly, social media actually tends to increase our feelings of outrage. Acts that would not elicit as much outrage offline elicit more online. This intensification may be due in part to the fact that the social benefits of expressing outrage online—such as increased tribal bonding—still exist and are possibly amplified, while the risks of expressing outrage are lessened (on the internet, it is harder for those you are yelling at to strike back with violence). Moreover, outrage can itself simply feel good. And since our digital platforms are designed to maximize shares and eyeballs on posts—and outrage does that—it is not surprising that the internet is a great mechanism for producing and encouraging the spread of outrage. As the neuroscientist Molly Crockett puts it, "If moral outrage is like fire, then social media is like gasoline."[16]

Put together, these points—what we are doing with our shares and what we are not doing—make it difficult to believe that the *primary function* of our communicative acts of sharing is really either assertion or endorsement, even though that's what we typically think we are doing.[17] By the "primary function" of a kind of communicative act, I mean that which explains why the act continues to persist. The primary function of yelling "Air ball!" at a basketball player trying to make a free throw is to distract him. It may do other things too—amuse people, or even describe what, in fact, turns out to be an air ball. But the reason people continue to yell "Air ball!" is that it is distracting. Someone new to the game could conceivably get this backward. They might think that people are warning the player or predicting how the shot is going to fall. Such interpretations would be misunderstanding the act's primary function.

Something like this is happening on a massive scale on social media. We are like the person just described, new to the game of basketball. We think "Air ball!" is meant to describe or predict. But it isn't. Put differently, we think we are playing by one set of rules—the rules of assertion and endorsement—when we are actually playing by a different set of rules altogether. We think we are sharing news stories in order to transfer knowledge, but much of the time we aren't really trying to do that at all—whatever we may consciously think. If we were, we would presumably have read the piece that we're sharing. But most of us don't. So, what are we doing?

A plausible hypothesis is that the primary function of our practice of sharing content online is to express our emotional attitudes. In particular, when it comes to political news stories, we often share them both to display our outrage—broadcast it—and to induce outrage in others. As Crockett has noted, expression of attitudes like moral outrage is one way that tribes are built and social norms enforced. Social media is an outrage factory. And paradoxically, it works because most folks aren't aware, *or don't want to be aware*, of this point. But *it is just this lack of awareness that trolls and other workers in the fake news industrial complex find so useful.* Purveyors of fake news are keenly aware that when we share, we're doing something different from what we think we're doing.

This is precisely where Hume's point, noted earlier, gets traction. As Hume and philosophers following him have often been at pains to illustrate, humans frequently misunderstand their own communicative acts. In ordinary speech, that's partly because the same words can be used to say, and do, very different kinds of things—to engage in different communicative acts. The sentence "I'm sorry" can mean "I apologize for what I did," or it can be used to simply express feelings of sympathy for someone experiencing a loss. Used that way, it is a bit like a consoling hand on the shoulder or the phrase "There, there." It is a way of signaling that we care. Given all the things we can do with words, it is not surprising that we can sometimes be confused. It is possible to use a medium of expression for one purpose when we think (and tell ourselves) we are using it for another.

In the middle of the twentieth century, one philosophical movement inspired by Hume diagnosed *all* of our moral thought and talk as falling into this category. Advocates of this view, appropriately called expressivism, argued that the purpose of moral language isn't to describe the world. Saying that the death penalty is wrong is not an attempt to describe some feature of the death penalty. It isn't like describing the weather as balmy. When we make moral judgments on this view, our real aim is to express our feelings and attitudes, in order to motivate others to feel similarly. As a result, it is a mistake, the expressivists argued, to think that an utterance like "the death penalty is wrong" is substantively true or false, because we aren't really aiming for it to be true in the first place. It is not an attempt (whether successful or not) to state a fact but a way of expressing ourselves and what we feel matters in the world. In some ways, it is more like saying, "Boo, death penalty!" Shouts of "Boo!" and "Yay!" aren't attempts to state facts at all; they convey emotion. By using them, we express ourselves, but we also hope to instill emotional reactions in others and strengthen the bonds between us. Knowledge and reason are not on our minds.

The original versions of expressivism, like a lot of philosophical views in their initial giddy moments of creation, overstepped. While it seems right that moral judgments are often a kind of self-expression, it seems just as likely that we can also (often at the same time) use them to describe what we think is really true. It is not an either/or situation. As a result, the original theories have been superseded by more nuanced views about the expressive aspects of moral communication.[18] Nonetheless, there is something clearly right about the view as well because, as Hume reminds us, we often do ignore the power of the heart in moral life. In any event, whether or not expressivism about all moral judgments is correct, it is a very plausible explanation for what is happening when we share content online. Indeed, it is especially plausible there, *for digital platforms are intentionally designed to convey emotional sentiment—because the designers of those platforms know that such sentiment is what increases reshares and ups the amount of attention a particular post gets. And whatever does that makes money.*

I am not saying that we don't endorse and assert facts on social media. Of course we do—just as some of us read what we share. Moreover, it is plausible to take ourselves to be endorsing or asserting *that part* of a shared post that we typically do read: the headline. As with shouts of "Air ball!" at a basketball game, our communicative acts online can do many things at once. But if you want to understand what I'm calling the *primary* function of a kind of communicative act, you need to look at the reason that the act continues to be performed. And in the case of sharing online content, that reason is the expression of emotional attitudes—particularly tribal attitudes. *Why?* Because expressions of tribal emotional attitudes like outrage are rewarded by the amount of shares and likes they elicit.

The expressivist account of online communication is also compatible with the fact that we do form beliefs and convictions as a result of sharing attitudes. Compare "team-building" exercises. These kinds of exercises (like falling back into your colleague's waiting arms) are not directly aimed at conveying information or changing your mind. They are aimed at building emotional bonds with your coworkers. But that, if all goes well, will have a downstream effect on what you believe. In learning to trust your team members, you will come to believe that this is the team you want to be on. A similar thing happens during the training of military recruits. Many of the exercises that new soldiers are put through are aimed at building trust and self-confidence. But especially in wartime, they are also aimed at making soldiers hate the enemy. This aim, too, has downstream effects: the soldiers come to believe they are fighting on the right side.

Social media is like boot camp for our convictions. It bolsters our confidence, increases trust in our cohort, and makes us loathe the enemy. But in doing so, it also makes us more vulnerable to manipulation and feeds our hardwired penchant for being know-it-alls. We think we are playing by the rules of rationality—appealing to evidence and data. But in fact, the rules we are playing by are those that govern our self-expressions and social interactions—the rules of the playground, the dating game, and the office watercooler. These rules have more to do with generating and receiving emotional reactions, solidifying tribal membership, and enlarging social status than with what is warranted by the evidence and what isn't.[19]

This emphasis on emotional reactions is perhaps most obvious on Facebook, whose stated goal, after all, is emotional connection. Consider how the platform encourages us to react to posts that we share with one another. It used to be that one could only "like" a post or refrain from liking it. But now Facebook offers the choice of a few different reactions, each corresponding to a basic emotion and represented by easily recognizable emoticons: frowny face, happy face, surprised face, and of course, angry outrage face. My experience in using these emoticons, which I suspect is widely reflected in others' use as well, is that they have a deep impact on how you think about the pieces being shared.

For one thing, the emoticons that other people in your network choose in reacting to a post can strongly affect how you yourself react. That effect is similar to the effects of social pressure offline. If everyone in your workplace dislikes something someone said or did, it is difficult not to show a similar reaction. Similarly, if your friends express outrage at a news piece, it can feel awkward not to do so yourself. And independently of that factor, the emoticon you choose can help condition how you comment on the post, if you do comment. If you choose the angry emoticon, for example, it is extremely unlikely that you will then comment by saying that the piece in question really made you think.

Now consider a thought experiment. Imagine that instead of the emoticons, we had a choice of three buttons that we could use when sharing a news story or other claim to fact: "justified by the evidence," "not justified by the evidence," and "need more information." How might having these choices—instead of emoticons aimed at the most basic human emotions—condition how we would engage with what we share and what we don't share?

One thought—no doubt overly hopeful—is that they would make at least some of us more reflective or thoughtful. We might even be less eager to share something we haven't read—because we would be thinking of people's reactions as being hinged not on their outrage or joy but more on the evidence they perceive the piece to communicate. It might encourage some of us to be more skeptical, and humbler, ourselves. But unless the basic digital economy changed, my hypothesis is that eventually, we would start treating all three buttons emotively. Eventually—as the old expressivists would have predicted—we would start to use the language of evidence to express feelings, not considered opinions. We could play on the emotions of others to get them to rate as "justified by the evidence" items that nonetheless go unread. And we might engage in spreading fake news and misleading evidence. So, not as much might be gained as we would wish.

Yet even if, in the way of thought experiments, this one is idealized, it highlights a crucial point. Just changing the surface appearances of our social-media platforms won't help. As long as we ignore the fact that their underlying economy rewards the expression of strong emotion over reflection, we will continue to deceive ourselves about the real nature of much of our communication on those platforms. We will continue to contribute, unwittingly or otherwise, to a corrupted information culture. And we will continue to make ourselves vulnerable to information polluters who revel in that corruption and take advantage of our naïveté, all the while complaining that our critics are peddling fake news.

3

✿

Where the Spade Turns

Why We Don't Change Our Minds

There is a certain tension in human life that most of us recognize, and that can cause us deep anxiety. That tension is between being open-minded and standing fast—between a willingness to change and having the courage of one's convictions. It is a tension we see play out on the political field—where an openness to change is generally an unwelcome attribute in politicians—even though most people want their governments to adapt to changing circumstances. But it also crops up in our personal lives anytime our fundamental commitments are challenged. For, the hard truth is that while we all like to think of ourselves as open-minded and intellectually humble, most of us find uncomfortable, or even morally problematic, the prospect of changing our minds about something that matters.

Sometimes shifting an opinion can even seem rationally impossible. There are times, the philosopher Ludwig Wittgenstein once noted, when reasons just run out, and "our spade is turned" on bedrock. That is how we often think of our deepest convictions—as the ground on which our worldview stands. They become part of the landscape, our frame of reference, our "picture of the world" that is the very "background against which [we] distinguish between what is true and what is false."[1] To reject them would be to completely change the picture, or maybe even erase it entirely, leaving us with no ability to know what is right, and what is wrong.

Wittgenstein was personally familiar with what it means to radically change your worldview. After all, this was the man who had declared that his first book, published in 1921 and amounting to something of an extended logical poem, had essentially solved all the problems of philosophy. The key, he thought, was understanding the secret logical structure of both thought and the world, on which all knowledge of any import must be based. Years later, he reversed himself and rejected his earlier work as being *itself* based on a fundamental misunderstanding of how language relates to the world and, indeed, of the point of philosophy itself.

Wittgenstein came to think that logical structure is less important than what we do with language, and he came to doubt the very possibility of grounding knowledge in the certainties of logic. In some of his last work, published posthumously, he insisted that the quest for philosophical justification always comes to an end—"but the end is not certain propositions' striking us immediately as true, i.e. it is not a kind of seeing on our part, it is our *acting*, which lies at the bottom."[2] What he thought we must learn to accept was the "groundlessness" of our beliefs.

Wittgenstein's remarks bring to the fore a fundamental problem in any attempt to grapple with dogmatism and arrogance in politics. As we've seen, social media can reinforce our natural penchant for self-certainty. But is it possible there is something deeper—something about the *very nature of conviction itself*—that makes us resistant to entertaining any idea that challenges our fundamental frames of reference? To what extent do we resist change not because of logic but because, as the later Wittgenstein might have said, we simply can't let go of our form of life?

What Kind of Person Are You?

The poet Ralph Waldo Emerson famously noted that nothing good was ever achieved without enthusiasm—and, one might add, nothing bad was ever accomplished without it either.[3] By "enthusiasm" here, Emerson presumably meant more than just joyful participation; he meant a motivating emotional commitment to what matters to us. That's a good approximation of what we mean by "conviction." Convictions are the wellsprings of action but the offspring of doctrine.[4] As any demagogue can tell you, to galvanize voters it helps to appeal to an ideology—namely, one people can identify with. What matters is getting voters to go beyond mere belief to total commitment.[5]

This is why there is an emotional component that comes along with conviction—what we call the "feeling of conviction." When directed at something you also believe, it is the feeling of self-confidence. It is a good feeling. It is good to be right, but it is also good to just feel as if you are right. That's why, for those of us worried about the fragile state of democracy, the old Yeats line still resonates: the "best" are often filled with self-doubt, while the worst are filled with the passion of conviction.[6] And it is also why it is important to understand why our convictions form in the first place.

Convictions feel certain. But not everything we feel certain about is a conviction. I don't *need* conviction for anything I'm absolutely or *logically* certain about. When René Descartes declared he was certain that he thinks and exists (popularly, but erroneously, understood as the inference "I think, therefore I am"), he meant he couldn't actively doubt he was thinking at that moment— because doubting is thinking. But it would be odd to say this was Descartes's *conviction*. Indeed, the interesting thing about convictions is that *they are often formed in the face of opposite convictions*. Unlike logical certainties like 2 and 2 make 4, or philosophical certainties like Descartes's belief in his own existence, we generally know that others may oppose our convictions. We are aware that our convictions can be doubted and challenged, even if we ourselves just cannot imagine that they are false.

Here, Wittgenstein seems on the right track: What *makes* a conviction a conviction is not its logical certainty or how well supported it is. It is not the content of the conviction that matters; what matters is its connections, or its perceived connections, to our way of life. Convictions aren't just beliefs we feel certain about. They are commitments to action.

To put it differently, our convictions signify to others what kind of person we take ourselves to be or aspire to be, and they reflect our self-image of being that kind of person. It is this fact that makes a conviction feel certain to us, whether or not it really is. Convictions are where attitude meets identity.

Identity is itself a Gordian knot. But this much we can say: the answer to "Who am I?" is a complex mix of internal and external factors. The external factors include those of history (for example, where my family came from), the environment (where I grew up), and biology (my genetics). But they also include the social groups I belong to (including my family), my ethnicity, my race, my gender, my sexual preference, and the role that I play in my social life. What kind of job I have, what sort of love life I enjoy, and how I interact with others all affect who I am and how I see myself. In short, much of what I am is partly the result of my *social identity*, as sociologists have long pointed out. But my overall identity—the kind of person I am—is also the result of internal psychological factors—my motivations, desires, hopes, fears, and the play and limits of my imagination. What philosophers like to call *personal identity* is often understood as built out of the continuity and connectedness of these psychological aspects—what Locke called consciousness. As John Locke emphasized, at least part of what makes me the same person as the boy in the photograph above my desk is that *I remember being that person*.

The aspect of overall identity that I am most concerned with here, however, is *self-identity*. My self-identity is determined by the interplay of the two internal and external kinds of factors just described, together with a third: what I care about, my values, and deepest commitments. Caring about something means identifying with it, investing in it to the point that I thrive when it flourishes and suffer when it is diminished.[7] And what I care about not only shapes the kind of person I aspire to be but signifies to others the kind of person I am. My values and commitments feed my own self-image—my representation, accurate or not, of myself in all three aspects of my overall identity: social, personal, and self.

One way to understand how my self-identity functions is to see it as my aspirational best self—as reflecting my deepest cares and commitments. I may desire to smoke; old habits die hard. But to the extent that I care about not being the kind of person who does—to the extent that I am committed to being healthier—I will sacrifice this desire and not smoke. Likewise, parents sacrifice many of their own goals for the sake of something that matters still more to them: the welfare of their children. Lovers sacrifice their needs for their beloved; activists, for their cause. It is a distinctive aspect of human beings that we can order our commitments in this way and regard ourselves as fully responsible—fully *together*—only when we end up acting in ways that reflect what we conceive to be our best selves.

The aspirational aspect of conviction captures the element of truth in the existentialist view that we choose our convictions; we decide on them. Jean-Paul Sartre thought we were "doomed" to be free to decide on our deepest moral beliefs. Taken literally, that idea seems implausible, for it ignores the fact that our convictions, like our other beliefs, often sweep over us and emerge out of histories we did not control.[8] This spontaneous emergence is apparent when we suddenly find ourselves having a conviction we did not know we had. But there is obviously some truth in Sartre's point as well. We often speak of *coming to decide* that something is right, or something is wrong. By this we mean that convictions are the commitments we would actively endorse as being central to who we are, were anyone to pose us the question.[9] We cannot control whether we believe or think that a particular proposition is deserving of our conviction. But what *is* under our control is our taking it up—our committing to it.[10] *A conviction is a commitment that reflects the kind of person we want to be.*

We often represent our aspirational visions of ourselves in an almost narrative form.[11] We structure our self-identity like a narrative—we see ourselves as having a beginning, a middle, and an end—but it is also *composed* like a narrative. We are storytelling creatures who tell the stories of ourselves to ourselves and to others. We can even see our self-narrative as having a plot of sorts; that is, we construct our self-narrative around the events and characters that have mattered to us and that guide our conception of the good.[12]

But the story of our self is not composed in the same way that Charles Dickens consciously plotted a story (the story of our teenage years: "It was the best of times; it was the worst of times"). For one thing, the narrative of our self-identity doesn't have just a single author. Our self-identity is our conception of our self, but it is also the result of stories told by others. Our parents tell all those embarrassing stories of when we were little; our friends tell all those stories about when we were in college. And of course, our self-stories are formed against the background of larger stories— cultural narratives that tell us what kind of people Americans or Europeans or South Koreans are; political narratives that tell us what kind of people Republicans or Democrats are; racial narratives that tell us what kind of people blacks and whites are; gender narratives that tell us what kind of people women and men are. Each of these cultural narratives has plot points of its own—elements that identify values and morally and politically significant events around which the rest of the story unfolds. By absorbing these narratives, we absorb the various moral prejudices and biases of our culture.[13]

This is not to say that every wider cultural narrative and every group membership is going to matter equally. For most people, whether or not they are members of AAA will not mean much for their conceptions of themselves.[14] The stories that matter are the stories we tell each other about the nature our tribe—about what kind of people we belong to, and what kind of people we don't. These are the stories that tell us what is sacred to us. The sociologist Arlie Russell Hochschild describes such narratives as "deep stories." As she puts it, a deep story is "a feels-as-if story—it's the story that feelings tell, in the language of symbols. It removes judgment. It removes fact. It tells us how things feel."[15] Hochschild's point is that our cultural narratives are shaped by and embody our attitudes.

This way of conceiving of self-identity helps us understand the nature of conviction. Convictions are those emotionally laden commitments that have become so woven into our self-narrative that they have become a part of our self-identity.

A simple way to illustrate this point is to conduct a thought experiment. Imagine that a scientist offers you a million dollars in exchange for a "conviction transplant." If you take the deal, you give up three of your deepest convictions and are "implanted" with their opposites. So you might, for example, become a committed racist, believe that your loved ones are unimportant dullards, lose your faith, and so on. Would you do it? I hope not. And, even if you did—thinking, for example, what the money might do for your loved ones—you'd probably see accepting the money as a significant sacrifice.

What explains our reactions here is that, when we are in the throes of conviction, we regard giving them up as a harm, precisely because we think of them as making us a certain kind of person. Indeed, some might think that losing their core convictions would mean they would cease to exist as the same individual; whoever survived the conviction transplant wouldn't be them, in other words. But even if we don't go that far, we are likely to think that losing our convictions will make our life a bit less worth living. And that sentiment tells us that our convictions signify to ourselves what kind of person we aspire to be.

Crucially, it works the other way around as well: we see other people's convictions as revealing who they are, and they in turn look at our convictions in the same way. Consider, to take a more realistic example, a religious couple worried that sending their daughter off to a secular college might cause her to lose her faith. Intuitively, their fear concerns their daughter's identity as religious. It is not about her existence per se; it is rather about the manner of her existence. The parents are afraid that their daughter will lose a belief of such fundamental value that she will no longer be the same kind of person. They may think that losing her religious faith will make her lose her moral compass; or they may simply feel that, even independently of morality, her religious convictions are part of who she is. We take our core convictions as both reflecting and constituting what kind of person we are—but we also use them as a way to measure other people's tribal identities. What makes you in or out of the group is often a matter of what you're committed to believing as much as what you do.

Because they reflect our self-identities, our convictions carry authority over our lives. Most obviously, they have authority over our actions; they obligate us to do some things and grant us permission to do others. A religious conviction, for example, can give believers the moral permission to blow themselves up, or cause them to engage in nonviolent protest in support of civil rights. Even a personal conviction can play this role—by excusing us, for example, from other moral demands. If one of your convictions is to put family before work, then it will make sense for you to skip a late meeting to make it to your kid's soccer game. Or, if you missed the last one, you might feel obligated to make the next one. We may not live up to such obligations, but we feel them just the same.

But convictions don't carry just moral authority. *They carry authority over what we believe.* Once something becomes a real conviction, it is difficult for us to doubt; it becomes part of our form of life.

Wittgenstein argued that certain propositions are like the hinges on which our worldview turns. On the surface, they can seem rather like any other proposition; they aren't special, mind-bending truths like Descartes's "I think, therefore I am," and thus they aren't certain in the logical sense. But we find it hard to really doubt such hinges anyway, because then the world would stop making sense. Consider, to take one of Wittgenstein's favorite examples, the proposition that I have hands. This *could* be false; it isn't like the thought that 2 and 2 make 4. But doubting that I have hands is not something I can ordinarily do with much seriousness. Anything I marshal to defeat the proposition will not be more certain than *it* is. Thus, attempts to convince me that I don't have hands, or that my name is not really Michael, would be met with extreme skepticism. Even if the evidence presented to me were very good (for example, evidence that what I thought was my birth certificate was a forgery), I might be inclined to think that the evidence, rather than my belief, was flawed. As Wittgenstein says, "Here a doubt would seem to drag everything with it and plunge it into chaos."[16]

Although they function in some ways like Wittgenstein's hinge propositions, convictions aren't generally about mundane matters that we typically take for granted or just believe without thinking about it. They are commitments. But we do hold convictions fixed, and we are willing to make all sorts of sacrifices on their behalf.

We often are willing to explain away contrary evidence, even if doing so flies in the face of the facts or logic itself. And we do that precisely because of the authority we give convictions over our life by virtue of their connection to our self-identity. That's why I am so reluctant to give them up, and why I may feel bad or guilty for not having the courage to live up to them. It is because they are commitments central to my self-identity that giving up a conviction can feel like an act of self-betrayal and a betrayal of one's tribe. And the tribe may well agree: if you don't share your tribe's convictions, you aren't a true believer, and that may mean having your membership privileges revoked.[17]

These facts are why it is so hard to be open-minded about our convictions, and why a challenge to our convictions can feel almost like an assault—an attack "on our way of life." Of course, we don't necessarily expect that people will agree with our convictions. But we do typically expect people to respect them, and to acknowledge our right to have them. These facts, in turn, explain why we are often unwilling to "go there"—to even discuss our convictions, as opposed to those beliefs that we think are true but we don't associate with our identity. Defending our convictions seems like defending our identity itself.

From Belief to Conviction

Friedrich Nietzsche, who probably thought more about convictions than any other philosopher, understood something about

convictions that is easy to overlook, yet crucial for understanding how they become the unwitting engines of arrogance. "Every
conviction has its history—its pre-formations, its ventures, its
mistakes," Nietzsche wrote; "it becomes a conviction only after
not being one."[18] What starts off as a simple belief, in other words,
can, given the right circumstances, take on all the pomp of a deep,
identity-reflecting value. And when that happens, the authority that the conviction brings with it—just by virtue of being a
conviction—means we may shield ourselves from evidence that
may seem to undermine it.

Nietzsche's point that convictions have histories as noncon-
victions helps to explain a particularly weird feature of much of
our public discourse right now—namely, that almost everything
can suddenly turn political. What you eat, the kind of car you
drive, and even where you buy your coffee are now commonly
seen as politically motivated choices. Thanks to the politicization
of climate change, even the weather is not off-limits. During the
late summer of 2017, under threat from an impending hurricane,
the governor of North Carolina ordered the evacuation of coastal
areas in the storm's path. Certain conservative talk show hosts
declared such hurricane hysteria to be part of a plot to bolster the
climate change hoax. Irrational? Absolutely. But such irrationality
is now sadly familiar. And much like claims that school-shooting
survivors are actors, such wild accusations don't just come out of
nowhere. In part, they reflect the growing sense that issues that
were once politics-free or off-limits are now seen through partisan lenses. And that shift in perception often happens precisely

because what we might call straightforward "matters of fact"—like whether a hurricane is threatening the coast, or whether Dunkin Donuts has "conservative" coffee—have been turned into matters of conviction. We've made them personal.

A "matter of fact" is a question that, at least in principle, can be decided by empirical means. Public debates often hinge on exactly such matters: whether a bridge project will cost this much or that much, whether more regulation will deter pollution, whether increased patrols in a neighborhood will lower the crime rate. These are the bread-and-butter issues of political policy, and they are not overtly philosophical matters. They are empirical ones, and we typically hope to bring to bear the tools of science to decide them. In the ideal world, we run the studies and then rely on the best view of the facts we have at the time to decide which way to go. But this ideal is often not realized. The process gets politicized, in at least one of two ways. One obvious means of politicizing an issue is to disagree about cost, and to engage in the usual and somewhat tiresome debate over government spending. Even in the face of such politicization, however, there is often widespread agreement about the facts, or at least about how they are to be investigated. The issue is really one about how best to construct policy in light of the facts.

But there is another way debates over matters of fact get politicized: they turn into matters of conviction. Consider the debate over climate change. On the face of it, questions about the causes of climate change are much like questions about the causes of damage to a bridge. But Americans do not approach the matter in the same way, as is indicated by research indicating that a person's political affiliations are highly predictive of an inclination to believe that climate change is a significant threat.[19] Conservatives are apt to think not; liberals are apt to think yes. Moreover, our political identities determine the extent to which we reject evidence that contradicts our views on climate change, or whether we are willing to accept even bad evidence that supports our worldview.

And that phenomenon is hardly contained to climate change. Would banning assault rifles reduce gun violence? Are vaccines safe? On all these issues, Americans are demonstrably prone to react to any data on the subject in a way that reflects their political viewpoint.

There are various ways to think about this problem. One might be that religiously influenced political viewpoints discourage scientific literacy. As a result, people reject climate change because they don't understand science in general. Solution: teach more science. Another is that some political approaches encourage close-mindedness and poor critical thinking skills more than others do. Solution: teach people logic.

Both of these suggestions have merit. There is good reason to think that people can, over time, become both more scientifically literate and better critical thinkers, at least in certain respects. Appreciating science is often more of a matter of coming to see that it is important to understand how something works, rather than to understand an abstract theory, for example. And we are more prone to think that it matters how something works when we can understand the stakes—such as the stakes of climate change. Moreover, people can, again over time, change their minds on matters of conviction—and reason can play a part. A good example on this score is people's attitudes on gay marriage. The shift in attitudes over the last decade is due to multiple factors. But one factor is the dramatic way in which court challenges to gay marriage have continually flopped—and flopped because of the inability of those challenging gay marriage to cite any evidence that it is harmful. The failure of the opponents of gay marriage here was, in this case, a rational and epistemic failure, and it arguably played a part in the larger cultural shift over time.[20]

Teaching critical thinking and science, however, is playing the long game. And on that score it is probably the most important approach. But in the short term these strategies often run smack into the fact that humans are prone to turn matters of fact into matters of conviction. And when that happens, we engage in identity-protective reasoning. That's because our convictions are part of our self-identity, our conception of our deepest self. And for that reason, the authority of conviction makes it very unlikely that teaching people more logic and science will help change their minds in the short run.

Recent research by Yale psychologist Dan Kahan and his colleagues makes the point vivid.[21] Kahan's work suggests that, contrary to common sense, the more scientifically literate and cognitively sharp you happen to be, the more polarized you often are—no matter what your political affiliation. Logically minded, scientifically literate conservatives are even more prone to dig in and defend their rejection of scientific studies supporting human involvement in climate change in the face of countervailing evidence. And the same is true of liberals opposed to vaccinations. The more you know, the more resistant you are to changing your mind. That stubbornness may be due in part to the fact that people who are more scientifically literate are more skilled at poking holes in studies they don't agree with, and at reading those they do agree with in the best possible light. But Kahan and others argue that this finding simply reflects a more general lesson: that we are prone to accept information when it affirms some aspect of our self-identity and to reject it when we perceive it as threatening that identity. And in one sense, this approach is practically rational.

Our understanding of the nature of conviction shows us that the point is entirely general. When we allow some matter of fact to become a matter of conviction—such as the human contributions to climate change, or the impact of gun control legislation on suicide rates, or the safety of vaccines—our commitments on these matters take on certain kinds of authority over our life. That's part of what makes them convictions. For that reason, it can become practically rational to ignore evidence that might undermine them. Convictions make it practically rational to be epistemically *ir*rational.

All this still leaves open the question of what causes us to turn matters of fact into matters of conviction in the first place. What makes us commit so deeply to a view about climate change or tax policy or veganism that we give it authority over our actions and beliefs?

One explanation, sometimes floated by Kahan, is peer pressure. Perhaps we turn ordinary beliefs into convictions when many people in our cohort start treating them that way. They become tribal badges of honor.[22] If you live in a community with mostly climate-change deniers—and more important, people for whom climate-change denial is a matter of conviction—it will be highly uncomfortable for you to be open to the reality of climate change. There will be social risks if you fight the current, and social rewards if you also deny climate change. So, there are powerful—if unconsciously operative—practical reasons for you to adopt climate-change skepticism as well.[23]

This explanation is a good start, but on its own it is neither necessary nor sufficient. It is not sufficient because peer pressure, when it is effective, also works at the level of mere belief in simple matters of fact. If my friends believe that the restaurant we're going to is open, I may on that basis adopt that belief as well, even if at first I doubt it. The same principle works for desires. The best way to sell something—to make people *want* to buy it—is to convince them that their peers want it too. So, while peer pressure and tribal cohesion explain why it is practically rational to want and believe what our peers want and believe, they don't explain how we turn a mere factual belief into a commitment that reflects our identity. And the fact that our cohort has a particular belief isn't necessary for a belief to become a conviction either. Otherwise we would never find examples of people who stood their ground against their peers. But of course we do.

To understand why beliefs become convictions, we need to

remember that they are commitments to what matters to us; they concern our *values*. Some of them are explicitly like that; they are explicitly about what is right and wrong. But that's not the only way we can acquire a commitment that we own as part of our identity. Straightforward matters of fact can become *morally entangled*. Matters of fact are the sorts of things we could assess, in some cases with scientific investigation, and in other cases with historical or legal or economic investigations. But as we've seen, certain matters of fact can be treated by people on both sides of the political spectrum as something that *must* be true (or false). When someone insists, for example, that climate change *must* be a hoax—or Trump *must* have personally conspired with Putin to get elected, the "must" is a signal that we have let a straightforward matter of fact become morally entangled.

Moral entanglement happens when one becomes committed to a belief in a matter of fact because its truth—rightly or wrongly—is regarded as evidentially related to a moral commitment, in the following sense: its falsity would undermine the perceived evidence for that moral commitment. When that happens, a seemingly straightforward claim about physical events has become shot through with our moral values. Thus, the empirical belief takes on moral salience from the explicit moral values around it, and any attack on it is treated as an attack on those values.

This is hardly a new phenomenon. Consider, by way of example, the nineteenth-century "scientific" belief in the differences in skulls between different races, which were thought to justify the belief that people of African descent were not only less intelligent than those of European descent, but literally of a different species, and thus could be treated unjustly or enslaved on that basis. Major scientific figures, such as the famed zoologist Louis Agassiz, were supporters of this view, and lectures given throughout the South were aimed to reinforce not a scientific viewpoint but a moral conviction—one that reinforced the image of the white southern male as genetically and morally superior. As a result, views about human anatomy became convictions.[24]

Or, to take an entirely different example, some Americans on the Left in the mid-twentieth century believed that the Soviet Union was misunderstood and more benign than their own government maintained. Some abandoned this belief in the face of news of Stalin's purges, gulags, and the brutal suppression of dissent in Czechoslovakia and elsewhere. But others rationalized away accounts of Soviet oppression. Their beliefs about historical events had become morally entangled in their overall views about justice and therefore became convictions themselves, super resistant to counterevidence.

We can see similar forces at work with regard to beliefs in the safety of vaccines, in the efficacy (or not) of free trade, and in the reality or unreality of climate change. The latter case in particular suggests that moral entanglement can work even when the explicit moral convictions are twice removed. Consider the claim made by some that climate change is a hoax perpetuated by the billionaire George Soros. If someone who believed this claim came to think it false, the shift in thinking probably wouldn't *directly* undermine any of that person's moral convictions. But it would have an indirect effect. For example, accepting that climate change is real would partially undermine the related belief that the scientific establishment is a propaganda arm of a liberal conspiracy. And that fact, in turn, *would* directly undermine the explicitly moral commitment that the scientific establishment is morally corrupt and thus not to be trusted.

Many, perhaps most, of our ordinary beliefs about the world are connected, if only distantly, with our moral principles (mathematical beliefs may be an exception). But that fact does not amount to moral entanglement. What I am calling moral entanglement is the process of coming to commit to a belief because it is perceived to have an evidential relationship to a strongly held moral conviction. That conception is consistent with the obvious fact that the process often goes the other way. Our commitments to matters of fact can cause us to develop certain moral convictions, as when a realization that opioid abuse is widespread makes someone come to view sentencing laws as unjust. That, too, could then count as moral entanglement, although it need not. Which things are morally entangled depends on the person.

Moral entanglement works with social pressure to act as a mechanism for instilling conviction. Many of our beliefs become convictions because they have already been woven into the larger narrative of a tribe we aspire to remain a part of. They become morally entangled because those beliefs reflect who we think we want to be; and our emotional commitment remains, no matter what challenges come down the pike. Indeed, *we take such challenges personally—literally, because we've expanded our self-identity, our self-narrative, to include the belief.* That is how an ordinary belief in a matter of fact becomes what we could call a "blind conviction." Blind convictions, like blind faith, are convictions formed not on the basis of evidence but on the basis of attitudes. We allow our self-identity, formed by our acceptance of wider cultural narratives and the attitudes they embody, to stretch and enlarge; it covers more ground and includes more as essential to it than it did before. Thanks to our unreflective desire to fit into wider narratives—to adopt them as our own—we take some matters of fact to be part of our identity, come what may.

If that assessment is right, then it raises an interesting and pressing question: if we can turn almost any belief into a blind conviction as a result of our desire to conform to preexisting cultural narratives, then what happens when it becomes super easy to share and shape those narratives? What happens when we carry around devices in our pockets that are essentially designed to do just that?

Our identities are not generally formed one by one. We construct the stories of our selves together, collectively. We just don't realize it most of the time. That's always been true, but it is especially so now, when the stories we tell ourselves about ourselves are increasingly being constructed in online social networks. For many of us, the kind of people we are is partly determined by our life online—what our social networks say about us, and what we say to them. Put differently, social-media platforms like Facebook are often used—either wittingly or unwittingly—as vehicles for self-expansion. Now we can see that they do so because they act as social reinforcement tools for moral entanglement. The platform is built to "connect us" emotionally—which, in practice, means it enables us to communicate our sentiments and attitudes to each other and to reward and punish each other for doing so. It is so good at it that it causes us to take up as commitments beliefs we may not have even thought about very much. As a result, we act on the policy that certain things are true even if we have no evidence to think they are. They must be true, we think, because—well, because that is what folks like us believe.

Earlier we saw that we are often ignorant about what we are doing on social media. We think we are exchanging information or knowledge—we are testifying to the credibility of something. But often we are not doing that at all. We are, without knowing it, expressing our emotional states and our attitudes. And that also makes it easy for social media to spur blind conviction. By sharing our outrage or our emotional attachment to some claim of fact, we signal to each other that the tribe must commit to it. We signal to each other that it should be a matter of conviction, that it should be part of our story. And we signal that it would be dangerous to change our minds. As a result, commitments that we think are principled, a result of our individual story of our best self, are actually just fragments of a larger cultural narrative. Social media can be a very effective blind-conviction machine.

In sum, to turn a belief into a conviction is to expand the self: we commit to beliefs as central to the narratives we identify with. And since those narratives concern what we value, beliefs that become convictions become morally entangled. Expanding the self and moral entanglement therefore tend to go hand in hand. Sometimes that expansion and entanglement is principled. Although we may not be correct at the end of the day, we commit to a belief because we come to see it as a moral matter of importance that the evidence supports. But often there's nothing principled about the way we arrive at our commitments. Often we allow the conviction machine of our online life to adopt commitments blindly. And unreflective adoption of commitments, in turn, leads to the sort of defensive, cognitive wall building associated with know-it-all arrogance. Intellectual arrogance is the result of confusing our self-esteem with truth. So, turning a matter of fact into a matter of conviction is always a danger. And when that happens blindly, on the basis of attitudes and not evidence, it feeds into a spiral of arrogance leading to more blind conviction leading to more arrogance.

We will need cognitive science to tell us about how the brain functions on conviction. The philosophically and politically important point is that when we are unaware that convictions can seem principled while actually being blind, we are helpless in the face of the conviction machine. And that helplessness makes our narratives—our very identities—vulnerable to being hijacked by those who feed off tribalism and transform conviction-inspired rage into an ideology of contempt and hate.

4

✹

Ideologies of Arrogance
and the American Right

Roots of Authoritarianism

The "amazing fact," wrote the German philosopher Hannah Arendt in 1945, after two world wars and the Holocaust, is not that a dictator's followers are willing to tolerate evil in his name. The amazing fact is that they don't waver even "when the monster begins to devour its own children."[1] This lack of concern for the interest of their citizens (on the part of the dictators) and for their own interest (on the part of the citizens) deeply puzzled rival states and outside observers at the time. "The fanaticism of members of totalitarian movements, so clearly different in quality from the greatest loyalty of members of ordinary parties, is produced by the lack of self-interest of masses who are quite prepared to sacrifice themselves."[2]

Arendt was concerned with specifically totalitarian movements such as fascism, but many of her observations apply to authoritarian states in general. She points out that outsiders' puzzlement about the motivations of authoritarian leaders can be strategically helpful to those leaders. In the case of Hitler, it made him unpredictable, simply because his reasons for doing things, and the reasons for his followers to go along, did not seem to make sense to many observers at the time. As Timothy Snyder, a historian of the Holocaust, has pointed out, one explanation for this unpredictability is that the Nazi movement in particular was not nationalist in a strict sense of that term.[3] That's because Nazi ideology wasn't geared toward, or motivated by, a typical liberal conception of national self-interest.[4]

Nazi ideology regarded national borders and institutions as tools to be used and then discarded when they were no longer needed. What was essential to Nazi ideology was blood (race) and soil (geography). The former marked the true divisions between the tribes of humanity; the latter referred to the idea that in order to prosper and feed themselves, racial tribes must compete for land. Once this racist ideology was accepted as a grand narrative, the standard economic models of the time—models that took it in the interest of nations to look out for the individual interests of their citizens—were less effective for understanding Nazi intentions.

The nature of Nazi ideology illustrates a general point about the psychology of authoritarian politics. Authoritarian rulers cultivate among members of the public two seemingly incompatible attitudes that nonetheless actually reinforce one another. The first is a feeling of defensiveness due to real or imagined persecution—the idea that somehow one's race or tribe or culture is under threat. In Hitler's eyes, "culture" meant Aryan culture, the tribe was the Aryan race, and the threat was a feared lack of land and food production. The other attitude is the felt sense of the tribe's inherent superiority—again, in Hitler's case, racial superiority. In almost all cases this superiority, racial or otherwise, is seen as emerging from history—a history whose secrets the dictator claims to have unveiled against the wishes of the enemy. Once this history is revealed, once the secret proclaimed, the people are told they will regain what was rightfully theirs all along. They only have to follow the leader.

This combination of perceived superiority and defensive insecurity provides a fertile psychosocial breeding ground for first resentment, and then hate. The attitudes naturally reinforce each other. Those who suffer from insecurity in the face of a perceived threat are prone to bolster their self-esteem by claims of superiority; those who claim superiority naturally regard those who disagree with them as a threat. Compounded many times and reinforced with the stirring power of a narrative, feelings of superiority combined with insecurity encourage not only racism and hostility but the more general idea that one's tribe has hold of both the true and the good, that it can't be wrong about what really matters, and that these facts should infuse policy and political action. It encourages, in other words, tribal arrogance.

People are attracted to arrogance. It is a powerful drug because it is so simple: it produces a feeling of power that requires no actual power, a feeling of knowledge that requires no knowledge. And it is easy to confuse arrogance with confidence, especially if you are feeling insecure and put upon. It is thus not surprising that ideologies built on tribal arrogance encourage loyalty, but not one based on content, as Arendt knew: "Total loyalty is possible only when fidelity is emptied of a concrete content, from which changes of mind might naturally arise."[5] Details only hem in those seeking tyrannical power. As Arendt notes, one of Hitler's greatest political achievements lay in overcoming the National Socialist Party platform, "not by changing or officially abolishing it, but simply refusing to talk about it or discuss its points."[6]

What was important, Hitler knew, was not having rational, detailed policies. Political power lay in stoking the combination of anxiety and perceived superiority, and hence the hateful arrogance of the tribe. That was the force that could cause members of the tribe to ignore an overreach of the dictator, even when he came to eat his own children. The point is not what ideas are presented but how they are presented, whether they resonate with the underlying attitudes and anxieties motivating the target public. As Arendt points out, "The form of infallible prediction in which these concepts were presented has become more important than their content."[7]

As specific content becomes less important, so does truth. Arendt is chillingly clear on this point: "The chief qualification of a mass leader has become unending infallibility; he can never admit an error."[8] For, to admit an error is to admit that there is something more powerful than you, that your triumph—and hence the movement's—may not be inevitable. As a consequence, she writes, speaking across the decades, "before mass leaders seize the power to fit reality to their lies, their propaganda is marked by its extreme contempt for facts as such, for in their opinion, fact depends entirely on the power of the man who can fabricate it."[9]

An ideology of arrogance is an ideology of the insecure and the defensive, and it is an ideology that at bottom must be hostile to truth, lest it wither in the face of the facts.

Telling It Like It Is

Arendt's analysis of the role of truth in authoritarian politics, and how those governed by such politics are willing to put their interests aside, is a universal thesis built on a historical example. Current American politics gives us other examples.

One of the puzzles of Donald Trump's rise in American politics is the overwhelming support he received from evangelical Christians during the 2016 campaign. That support mystified commentators on the Left and more than a few evangelicals themselves, since Trump seems to represent the very opposite of Christian values: greed, intolerance, selfishness, and a lack of humility. Not to mention that for much of his career he had taken stances on issues like abortion and gay marriage far from those found in typical conservative Christian circles. Nonetheless, the support was there, and real.

It is this puzzlement that evangelical writer Stephen Strang set out to address in his 2017 book *God and Donald Trump*. Strang, a publisher and CEO of Charisma Media (which published the book) campaigned for Trump; his bio on the book's jacket even proclaims that he attended the "election night victory party in New York." The book's unsubtle subtext is that the very fact that so many mainstream Republicans and liberals *were* puzzled about evangelical support for Trump is one reason he won the election. The "dominant progressive culture," Strang says, missed the point, and thereby displayed its basic ignorance of both the evangelical movement and many American voters.

Strang's explanation for why evangelicals supported Trump comes in two parts. The first part is a now-familiar cultural narrative. Trump understood the "deep resentment of the men and women in the flyover zones who felt their country was being ripped from their fingers and their moral heritage being squandered."[10] These voters, writes Strang, "were tired of the government's lurch towards globalism in the Obama administration. They were concerned about the impact undocumented immigrants were having in their communities and they were rightfully afraid of the threat of radical Islamic Terrorism."[11] Early on in the campaign, Strang writes, he came to "believe Donald Trump shared those emotions," although he confesses to having been worried as to how much was a matter of "tactics" and how much was "genuine concern for the future of the nation."[12]

Nonetheless, throughout the book Strang makes the case that for many evangelicals, the important thing about Trump was not whether he shared their faith per se, or even whether he shared all the same values. As Strang himself admits, while he *thinks* Trump is a Christian, it is not clear that Trump understands the difference between evangelical Christianity and mainline Protestantism.[13] The important thing, says Strang, is that Trump "tells it like it is"—even when, and especially when—"the way it is" is unpopular on the Left. In a telling passage, Strang discusses Trump's speech at the 2016 Republican National Convention—the speech in which he famously declared that the nation was in crisis, that crime was running rampant, and that "nobody knows the system better than me, which is why I alone can fix it." To the mainstream media, Strang notes, the speech was darkly dystopian; but to "those who agreed with Trump's vision for America . . . his words were encouraging, largely because someone was finally speaking the truth."[14]

Aristotle famously (and rightly) said that to speak the truth is to say of what is, that it is, and of what is not, that it is not. Understood that way, the idea that Trump excels at truth telling is, well, bizarre. He is willing to say almost anything and is notoriously untethered from the facts. (This is the man, after all, who gave a rambling, inappropriate speech to the Boy Scouts of America and then—in the face of direct denials by the organization's leader and his desperate attempts to distance the organization from the speech—declared they had told him "it was the greatest speech ever made to them.") So rather than arguing the point, we should be asking what is meant by phrases like "he tells it like it is" or "he speaks the truth" when used in this sort of context.

There are at least two salient interpretations. Understood one way, for example, to say of someone that they "speak the truth" is to say not that they describe the objective facts, but that they are willing to speak of what is momentous and hidden and to do so no matter what the consequences. This is the revelatory use of the phrase "tells it like it is." And many Trump supporters do see Trump as willing to state what they think of as momentous hidden "facts"—such as that climate change is a hoax, or that immigrants are taking over the country—which those in the "mainstream media" are not willing to take seriously. Such views are momentous in that those who hold them perceive them to be of grave, possibly even sacred, importance; but they are hidden in that—again, in the eyes of those who hold them—they've been deliberately obscured or ignored.

Another use of the phrase "tells it like it is" is what we might call the emotional use. Telling it like it is or speaking the truth can also mean saying what you *feel*. The "it" that one tells here is not the world but oneself. And what attracts some, perhaps many, of Trump's supporters is not *what* he says, but his expression of anger, resentment, and supreme confidence when he says it. There is no apology for those feelings, no backing down. *That* is what many people are responding to when they say that Trump speaks the truth. It is not the content of his views but *the feelings he gives voice to—feelings that they think have been denied or that they have been belittled for experiencing.* As the sociologist Arlie Russell Hochschild notes, Trump's ability to give voice to shared emotional truth often elated his followers in a way that cemented tribal loyalty. It was the elation of having one's attitudes validated.

And the "desire to hold on to this elation became a matter of emotional self-interest."[15] Voting for Trump, in this view, wasn't just a matter of supporting someone with the right policies or even the right values. It was supporting someone who shared their attitudes and was willing to publicly express them.

This basic ambiguity of phrases like "tells it like it is"—trading between "uncovering the hidden facts" and "saying what you really feel"—often goes unnoticed by those on the Left. But the emotional and the revelatory uses help to explain why this phrase resonates with Trump supporters. It also helps to explain why so many of them seem, at least to their opponents, to be immune from the facts. If you distrust the media and scientific institutions, it is not surprising that citing media sources and scientific evidence is not going to be persuasive. But it is also not surprising that you'll think that the media is obscuring deep "truths." For it is the nature of "hidden facts" that they are bound to fly in the face of more widely accepted truths. Moreover, because cultural narratives embody our attitudes, and those narratives can, in turn, determine the convictions that form our self-identity, the validation of your attitudes and feelings means the validation of that identity. To those who share these attitudes and the convictions that go with them, "telling it like it is" means giving voice to that identity. Evidence is beside the point, and citing facts will just seem like an attack on one's identity.

Crucially, Strang makes just this point himself. As noted, he emphasizes the importance of Trump "sharing emotions" right from the outset; the worry is not whether Trump shares a policy vision, but whether he is being emotionally authentic. But as I've noted, Strang also adds a second part to his argument: an explicitly theological explanation of why it made sense for evangelicals to support Trump. He quotes former Watergate conspirator and now evangelical minister Chuck Colson's idea of "common grace." As Strang explains it, "A key aspect of the concept holds that secular leaders are raised up in times of great historical consequence to protect God's agenda and His purposes. Such leaders are chosen for a unique role, whether or not they may actually know God or even care about doing His will."[16]

This, Strang suggests, is precisely what has happened to Trump. He has been chosen by God, and it shouldn't really matter to evangelicals whether Trump is a Christian or has Christian values. The point is that he has been chosen to lead his supporters to power. To think otherwise is to ignore the common grace that God has given in his mercy. So, it is perhaps not surprising that Strang brings out his greatest invectives for Christian leaders like the Southern Baptist Russell Moore, who vocally opposed Trump during the campaign. Opposing Trump, Strang thinks, is tantamount to opposing the will of God.

The Logic of Status Threat

The question of why so many evangelicals supported Trump is just one instance of a larger question, one that was of clear interest to Arendt: why people support authoritarian leaders even when—

and especially when—they are "willing to devour their own children." Strang's kind of answer, as we've seen, is solidly cultural, religious, and psychological, not economic. It is about identity and attitude, not money.

To some, however, this kind of explanation rings false for just this reason, particularly in the case of Trump. According to this counternarrative, the real reason people wanted to support Trump, the real reason they wanted to burn the house down, was not because he validated their attitudes, but because they are fundamentally frustrated with an economic system rife with inequality—a system that has rewarded coastal elites and left the rest of what coastal elites refer to as "flyover country" behind.

This economic explanation features prominently in a general and ongoing debate over strategy on the Left. According to one side of the debate, represented by political analyst Thomas Frank and others, a major reason that the Democrats lost the 2016 presidential election is that they assumed people were supporting Trump only out of racism or sexism.[17] The thought is that this assumption led to two fundamental errors. First, by dismissing Trump voters as "deplorables"—to use Hillary Clinton's notorious phrasing—progressives displayed an arrogant moral superiority that only served to galvanize the opposition.[18] Second, by focusing solely on racist and sexist motivations, Democrats missed the single issue that galvanized followers of both Trump and Sanders: an economic power structure that benefits the elite over the vast majority of the working class. On this reading, Trump supporters were motivated to vote primarily because of economic class, not because of race, sex, gender, or other cultural issues. And ignoring that fact, according to this line of thought, continues to make the Left vulnerable.

There is no doubt that many Americans view those on the Left as arrogant know-it-alls looking down their nose at the rest of the country. Moreover, and as we'll see later, there is more than an element of truth to this charge—although not, perhaps, for the reasons that some have thought. But the point I wish to make here is simpler—namely, that much of the debate over the 2016 election rests on the assumption that we must choose between either culture or the economy to explain why so much of white America voted for Trump. That is a false dilemma. There is a third choice: that the cultural and the economic explanations, both of which capture an element of the truth, are in fact *different expressions of a more general fact*. And interestingly, it is a fact that Strang's analysis clearly supports as being explanatory: that many white Christian males voted for Trump because they felt that, in cultural and/or economic ways, the "American way of life" was under attack and they feared a perceived loss of status that would result.

The political scientist Diana Mutz has collected data over a wide-ranging series of studies that points to just this fact. Perceived threats to the "American way of life," her studies show, were a reliable indicator of support for Trump in the 2016 election.[19] In essence, Mutz argues, white Christian Americans who felt a threat to (1) their status in society and/or (2) the nation's status in the world were most likely not only to vote for Trump but to do so even if they had previously voted Democratic. And significantly, the studies suggest that many of these voters had felt neither sort of status threat during previous elections. They had acquired one or both types over the last few years.

This point is important for two reasons. First, it goes against the received wisdom that political campaigns can't (at least generally) give people new motivations to vote, but just make their existing motivations more salient ("It's the economy, stupid!"). It suggests that the Trump campaign actually did succeed in motivating at least some voters in a new way: by encouraging fear of a loss of personal or national status. Second, it helps to explain why those voters who newly came to these motivations would vote for Trump. What it suggests, Mutz argues, is that people who came to experience status threat—who, in other words, were increasingly convinced of a threat to either personal status or national status—were prone to support the candidate who emphasized reestablishment of past hierarchies. For white people who were suddenly fearful, for example, that they were soon not going to be in the racial majority, or that whites were more discriminated against in the United States than blacks (yes, some people believe that), a candidate who promised to "make America great again" was intuitively appealing.

The crucial point here is that the status-threat explanation is consistent with the perceived threats coming from different sources. For some people, the greatest perceived threat may indeed be racial: fear of a future in which whites are no longer a majority of the population. For others, it might include gender-based fears: the fear by men of being supplanted by women in power roles.

For others, that threat might, as the "left-behind" thesis suggests, be economic: the fear that global trade policies are undermining America's ability to compete with other countries and thus maintain its status as the strongest economy in the world—an economy with stable jobs for, among others, white males. For still others, the perceived threat might consist in the fear that Christian values are no longer dominating discussions in the public sphere. Or it might be a combination of all of these.

What links these fears, what makes them similar, is that they are each, in their different way, a reaction to a real or perceived threat to the cultural status of certain interlocking groups of voters. And Mutz's point—and I think, interestingly, also Strang's—is that this threat to status is what matters most, for the simple reason that, as her data suggests, its presence continues to predict support for Trump whether or not, for example, one has experienced economic hardship or personally felt discriminated against as a white person.

Status threat does not require the kind of overt racism or sexism consisting of explicit beliefs that minorities or women are morally or intellectually inferior. Most Trump voters indignantly reject the idea that they are racist or sexist in this overt sense—and rightly point out that they are no more overtly racist or sexist than are many liberals.[20] *Overt* racism and sexism can be beside the point when it comes to status threat. Threats to racial status can be felt simply on the basis of more subtle kinds negative racial, religious, or gender attitudes—for example, the perception that women or minorities are "sufficiently powerful to be a threat to the status quo."[21] As Mutz's research reveals, the same "individuals who perceive whites as more discriminated against than minorities also see Christians and men as experiencing greater discrimination than Muslims or women, despite the former groups' dominant status."[22]

During the Trump campaign, these feelings were brilliantly distilled not only by "Make America Great Again" but by "America First," which turned out to be another usefully ambiguous slogan. Initially, commentators treated it as expressing a simple isolationist mind-set—an endorsement of the policy that elected officials should look after the national interest, and should put it above the interests of other nations (perhaps, as some have thought, because the United States is "exceptional" or "historically unique"). But for Trump and many of his most ardent followers, the "first" in "America First" means simply "the winner" or "the best."

Understood in this way, "America First" doesn't state a policy; it expresses an attitude: that America is superior—not just as a matter of contingent historical fact, but *intrinsically*. The nation is tarnished, perhaps, by years of Democratic leadership, and in need of a bit of Trumpian polish to let its gold leaf shine through; but it is the best, the most winning, just the same. To understand the phrase "America First" in this way is to see it, like "tells it like it is," as emotionally expressive—not an endorsement or statement in any intellectual sense; it expresses an attitude that has, paradoxically, become more entrenched in American culture even as events make it harder to rationally justify. And the attitude extends beyond just the political realm—all the way, for many whites, to cultural identity itself. America's true greatness lies in its having created the greatest way of life that could *ever* be—a way seen hazily in beer commercials, in which white Christian Americans play a privileged part. A threat to that image—whether real or just perceived—therefore creates anxiety.

This kind of anxiety can itself encourage resentment. Hochschild offers a perceptive analogy. It is as if conservative whites in the United States see themselves as having been patiently waiting in line for the American dream. But as they wait, they hear that other people—many of them looking very different from them—are "cutting in line." Moreover, various people far ahead of them in line—richer people who live on the coasts, perhaps—are holding spots for these other, browner people. Seeing this, they seethe with resentment. And they seethe even more when people farther up in line tell them to stop feeling resentment. By this analysis, Trump is like a person already at the head of the line who calls back and validates your feelings and promises to hold *your place* in the line and to prevent line cutters from taking that place away from you. It doesn't matter that he isn't much like you—that he is, in fact, more like the people you resent. Indeed, it helps; that's what gets him his place farther up the line.

The analogy with standing in line is illuminating for several different reasons. It helps to explain the kind of resentment at play among many supporters of Trump in this country. And it explains the willingness to believe Trump's repeated insistence that his wealth is what makes him the best man for the job—because if the job is reaching back and helping largely white voters to cut in line, it does.

ARROGANCE AND THE AMERICAN RIGHT

But there is another point here, not emphasized by Hochschild but suggested by the analogy of the line cutter: Trump voters' resentment stems from the perception that they have lost their *rightful* place farther up the line. If you know (or think you do) that you *deserve* to be farther up the line than you are, then of course you'll feel angry at anyone ahead of you, and you'll look for explanations. And you'll put tremendous stock in those explanations, treating them not just as guesses, or even just as beliefs. They'll become convictions, part of your self-identity. When people criticize you for holding them and for being resentful, you'll be defensive. It will seem like you are under attack, like people are telling you what to feel. But the idea that you've lost your rightful place in line assumes *that there was such a thing as a "rightful" place to begin with.* The idea that there are rightful starting places, and that some people have one that is farther ahead than other people who are not white, is one of the oldest racial tropes there is—and one of the most dangerous. When liberals criticize Trump voters' resentment, they are reacting to that trope. They are saying that white people shouldn't feel resentment *because they are white.*

Naturally, that is not how many Trump voters regard the basis of their resentment. They've worked for what they have. They should be farther along than they are. These are reasonable views, and thus, as we've noted, it is entirely reasonable to think that income inequality also generates status threat—either on its own or mixed up with racial fears. What's important is not to fall into thinking that it is either just identity/cultural issues or the economy that explains white support for Trump. The better

91

explanation points to attitudes that both issues can encourage. And tellingly, the sociological analysis (from the outside) dovetails with Strang's analysis (from the inside) of why Trump voters are filled with resentment and anxiety. The point in both cases is that many whites supporting Trump do so because of their attitudes— because they fear they've lost their rightful place in line and are anxious and angry because of that fear.

These very attitudes, together with the internal logic of status-threat anxiety, feed authoritarian politics. Arendt is clear on this point: "Politically speaking, tribal nationalism always insists that its own people are surrounded by 'a world of enemies,' 'one against all,' that a fundamental difference exists between this people and all others." Yet at the same time, "it claims its people to be unique, individual, incompatible with all others."[23] In other words, the language of nationalism is a language that speaks to status anxiety; it is the language of tribal arrogance.

Arrogance, Ignorance, and Contempt

I want to be clear about the arguments I am, and am not, making here. What I've been arguing is that the rise of nationalism and authoritarian politics is often related to the rise of a widely shared defensive psychosocial attitude—status threat. Status threat, I've claimed, is explanatorily distinct, but often stems from, either economic fears or racist fears or both. Those who feel status threat are apt to identify with political ideologies and narratives that encourage tribal arrogance, that promise a return to greatness, and that remind them they are really superior and deserve to be at the head of the line. And as Arendt has pointed out, such ideologies of arrogance are deeply dangerous.

What I'm *not* saying is that all conservative-leaning Americans have actively embraced this political viewpoint or feel status threat to begin with. The existence of conservative resistors to Trump—both within and without the administration—should make that obvious. Many conservative intellectuals—from Ross Douthat, to David Brooks, to Arthur Brooks and Jonah Goldberg—have been keen to distinguish political conservatism from the nationalist politics defended by Trump and his followers. Indeed, the distinction between more traditional conservatism and the ideologies of arrogance that I've been discussing is crucial, because we are still in the midst of a battle over cultural narratives. It behooves both sides of any war—literal or cultural—to declare that everyone is firmly committed to one side or the other. But that is almost never the case. Rather, many people will only lean slightly one way or the other. So if you want to win the culture war, or even defuse it, you need to understand that fact; you need to realize that the war is fought in the trenches of conviction. That is, it is fought over whose narratives can turn weakly held beliefs into strong convictions.

As opposed to middle-of-the-road conservatives, many on the far Right, I think, see this very clearly. They have sucked the nectar of arrogance and embrace its distortion of truth as a friend. A good example is the kind of conspiracy theory that pops up after virtually any act of violence associated with ultra-conservative causes. In Chapter 2 we saw one such conspiracy—Pizzagate—but an even better example for present purposes is the one that sprang up immediately following the August 2017 events in Charlottesville.

In the second week of that month, neo-Nazis marched on the University of Virginia campus, shouting, "Jews will not replace us" and "Blood and Soil" (a historical Nazi slogan). They were there ostensibly to protest plans by the city of Charlottesville to remove a memorial to Robert E. Lee. The next day a white man drove his Dodge into a crowd of counterprotestors, killing thirty-two-year-old antiracism protestor Heather Heyer. Almost immediately following these events, it was reported that Alex Jones of Infowars suggested that the murder and, indeed, the "Unite the Right" rally itself were actually staged "false-flag" attacks coordinated by the "deep state" and (Jewish) billionaire George Soros.[24] The neo-Nazis were actually paid actors, Jones was reported to have claimed, as was the man who used his car as a murder weapon. To the surprise of no one, this theory spread throughout the dark corners of the internet, but it was also picked up by more mainstream voices, including several Republican congressmen. Arizona Representative Paul Gosar, for example, was reported to have said in an interview, "Maybe [the rally] was created by the left" and, in another interview, "proof will be coming" that Soros was behind Unite the Right.[25]

This is all weird enough; the claim, after all, is that liberal activists would pose as Nazis and then kill one of their own under the same pretension. But it is just one instance of a far-Right political strategy that explicitly fans the flames of a wider cultural narrative about monuments to white soldiers who fought on behalf of the Confederacy. To many whites in the South, these statues represent not only their heritage but that of the whole region. But to others—including African Americans whose ancestors were slaves—these same statues celebrate a cultural and political movement that protected, and indeed fought for, slavery. The debate showcases the overall point of the last two chapters: that blind convictions form as a result of larger cultural narratives and that political ideologies can push people into acting on behalf of these narratives—often violently. What the advocacy on the far Right of conspiracy theories shows is that these ideologically fueled narratives work in part by encouraging narratives of tribal arrogance—a sense of certainty about the nature of the world that excuses *and indeed, encourages, distortions of obvious facts.*

We can begin to unpack this claim by examining the attitude of intellectual arrogance—and especially tribal arrogance—in more detail.

As I noted at the outset of this book, arrogance isn't simply about misjudging self-worth; it is based on a self-delusion about *its basis.* While the intellectually arrogant think their felt superiority is due to their knowledge, it actually reflects a defensive concern for their *self-esteem.*

This delusion is at work in tribal arrogance as well. Tribal arrogance is typically directed at *specific* groups and the sources of information that are associated with those groups. As a result, someone who is arrogant toward African Americans and Latino immigrants will dismiss sources perceived to be friendly to those groups—for example, CNN and the *New York Times*—as "fake news." And just as someone can be arrogant *toward* a group, one can be arrogant *because of* a group. In other words, people can be arrogant about their narratives and convictions *because having them is thought to be essential* to being in a group they identify with. Beliefs that are central to the group's shared identity become part of its cultural narrative. They become immune from revision and protected at all costs from counterevidence.

The delusion at the heart of arrogance has two faces. The first face is epistemological. The tribally arrogant believe that their confidence in their own superiority stems from the fact that they are just smarter, more credible, and more knowledgeable than their opponents. But as with those that embrace false-flag conspiracies, their unwillingness to take obvious evidence seriously is more likely to stem from a defensive protection of a cultural narrative they identify with. This unwillingness, when expressed as a form of widely shared tribal arrogance, results in a kind of willful ignorance—a systematic and coordinated refusal to acknowledge evidence.[26]

Such active ignorance isn't just operating at the level of conspiracy theories. It also operates at the level of the more general cultural clash over Civil War monuments. This clash, as both sides clearly know, is not really about old stone statues; it is over history itself. For many white defenders of those monuments, the issue isn't merely recognizing the historical facts, or even the physical bravery, of whites who fought for the South. That there's more to the issue is evidenced by the fact that, for these defenders of the monuments, placing them in the context of a museum is not acceptable. The fight is over what Yale philosopher Jason Stanley usefully describes as the "mythic past"—an active rewriting of Civil War history that downplays both the role of slavery in the causes of the war and the racism of those whites who worked to undermine Reconstruction.[27]

The second face of the delusion is moral.[28] Tribal intellectual arrogance isn't just about "us" versus "them." It is about "us" *over* "them." This fact is most apparent in the tribal arrogance of racism, since racists think not only that they are superior to other races but that the others are somehow at fault.[29] People can be tribally arrogant but not racist, but it is difficult for them to be racist without, at least on some level, being tribally arrogant— without thinking, in other words, that their capacities for knowledge are superior and that they are to be morally commended, and the others morally blamed, for this fact. This holds generally for the intellectually arrogant, whether their arrogance is racist or not: their knowledge is superior, they know the secret truths. And they think this means that their humanity, too, is *morally superior*. They are better people because they know what's what; the "others" are responsible for just not keeping up. That's why tribal arrogance brings contempt in its wake. To be contemptuous about others' beliefs—for example, their religious beliefs—is to see them as rationally inferior, or unworthy in certain respects, and to see those who have those beliefs as perhaps feebleminded or deluded or both.

Put together, the two faces of delusion at work in tribal arrogance constitute something similar to Sartre's bad faith—a lived denial of the evidence that is made all the easier by the pollution and corruption of the information environment.[30] Such corruption creates an environment in which almost anything can be taken seriously; almost any claim, no matter how crazy, can be found credible. That corrupt information environment, in turn, makes it possible to be both gullible and cynical at the same time—in precisely the way we often see manifested online in the sorts of conspiracy theories that propagate there. The combination of gullibility and cynicism enables bad faith on a massive scale—a scale particularly useful to authoritarian leaders looking to promote ideologies of arrogance. As Arendt notes, "Under such conditions, one could make people believe the most fantastic statements one day, and trust that if the next day they were given irrefutable proof of their falsehood, they would take refuge in cynicism; instead of deserting the leaders who had lied to them, they would protest that they had known all along that the statement was a lie and would admire the leaders for their superior tactical cleverness."[31]

Yet the bad faith at the heart of intellectual arrogance can stretch even beyond the ignoring of evidence. Arrogance distorts our relationship to truth itself. When we fall victim to it, we fall victim to the idea that, to some extent, *our worldview is correct just because it is ours.*

There are two things this can mean. First, it might mean an equation of ego with truth. That often happens, as Arendt pointed out, in the case of authoritarian leaders. If a leader believes that the correctness of his views consists in their truth, then he may act as if his beliefs are true just because he has them.[32] It is as if he thinks he's a god; he thinks that if he believes p, then p. Note that this doesn't mean he can't change his mind, or that if he believes p then he must always believe p. What it does mean (assuming classical negation) is that if not p, then he does not believe p, and if he comes to believe not p, then not p. The divine may change his mind, but when he does, reality changes too.[33] This is a bizarre conception of truth, and no one could hold it coherently. But I never said intellectual arrogance makes sense.

Yet this is not the only way, and probably not the most common way that extreme intellectual arrogance pops up in our lives—or in authoritarian leaders. The second way arrogance can distort one's relationship to truth stems from not caring about truth in the first place. For certain people, especially certain powerful people, what matters—what, in their view, makes their opinions correct—is not that they have a hold on the truth but that they have power, or brilliance, or wealth. What matters is something else, something connected to their self-esteem. Bad faith toward the truth works at the tribal level too. It can encourage the thought that if the relevant group or community is convinced of something, then it is true. Or it may be that the truth of the matter is simply unimportant or ignored. What matters is group loyalty. Might makes right, and truth is irrelevant.

It is worth noting that the bad faith at work in arrogance means that it is more than just simple close-mindedness.[34] You can end up being close-minded without identifying with a larger cultural narrative or being defensive about its truth. You might just be surrounded by information pollution, or lack critical thinking skills or the relevant concepts, or live where government prevents people, perhaps via censorship, from engaging in debate. Arrogance, on the other hand, is dogmatic close-mindedness that stems from bad faith, from a delusion about the basis of one's confidence.

Over the last few chapters, I've been arguing that our lives online and off encourage our natural inclination to think that we—that is, those who share our identities and convictions—have figured it all out, that we know it all. Our use of social media, for example, exploits tribal anxieties and attitudes that can feed intellectual arrogance. Attitudes like arrogance, in turn, become cemented into our narratives and blind convictions. The result is a cycle of sorts: attitudes like intellectual arrogance are embodied by convictions, which themselves encourage those attitudes.

The point I've been making in the last few pages is that certain political ideologies play into this cycle: they speed it up by shaping the narratives that turn beliefs into blind convictions and, in turn, both reflect and encourage intellectual arrogance. They do so, we've found, in four main ways. First, the ideologies of arrogance exploit the natural and perfectly normal human desire for status and shared identity; second, they encourage loyalty to the tribe at all costs; third, they are hierarchical and adopt a politics of "us" over "them"; and fourth, they express a distorted and self-deceptive view of truth and its importance.

Strang and Arendt teach us that ideologies of arrogance can bear no counterexamples. If you believe in your inherent moral superiority, then mistakes must be defensively denied or explained away. That's not surprising: arrogance is often a compensation for something—a perceived failure or loss—and as we've seen, it brings with it self-defensiveness, which brooks no admission of error. Recent battles over immigration, health care, and climate change illustrate this essential character of arrogance. Because of a real or perceived threat to an ideology of cultural or racial entitlement, many people are willing to follow conviction over the facts, to hold that these are problems caused not by Americans but by others, and the right prescription is to build a wall of purity between us. While these cases are important in themselves, taken together over the last decade they have had a snowball effect. They've caused many white Americans not to become more open or tolerant but to dig in on their beliefs, to denounce those who see room for cultural improvement—whether that be in terms of race relations or health care or transgender rights—as traitors to the very idea of the "real America."

5

❈

Liberalism and the Philosophy
of Identity Politics

Arrogant Liberals

A young progressive I know was frustrated with his parents' refusal to talk about politics with him and his partner. After repeated attempts, his mother finally told him why: his parents didn't want to talk politics with the young couple because they found them to be insufferable, arrogant, liberal know-it-alls, and regarded the prospect as exhausting.

It's easy to sympathize; talking politics with your children—or your parents, for that matter—*can* be exhausting, no matter what side of the political spectrum you find yourself on. But this example also illustrates a simple fact about the American political landscape today: liberals are largely perceived, sometimes even by themselves, as arrogant and disdainful of those on the other side. Conservapedia, which bills itself as an alternative to Wikipedia, even has an entry for "liberal arrogance," defined as the "tendency of liberals, in their unwarranted pride, to make presumptuous assumptions." Google this topic, or roam around social media, and you'll find lots of pieces that talk about liberals as intolerant, smug, and disdainful. And those are the polite words.

Most of my fellow liberals are apt to shrug their shoulders at this. Sticks and stones, they say; after all, reflection and open-mindedness are core liberal virtues. The fact that others don't appreciate our virtuousness, or project their own arrogant attitudes onto our values, is their problem, not ours.

Indeed, but one might wonder whether that reaction is part of the problem. Perhaps we should first ask: What, if anything, about progressive political philosophy encourages this association with arrogance?

As it turns out, the explanation is both simpler and more complicated than is often thought.

Misunderstanding the Politics of Identity

Perhaps the most commonly cited cause of progressive arrogance is identity politics. And identity politics, the thought goes, is very bad indeed. Among other things, we are told that it exploits "divisions between people,"[1] is "poisonous to the American miracle,"[2] and is responsible for leaving an entire generation "unprepared to think about the common good and what must be done practically to secure it."[3] Identity politics, according to this construal, undermines not only traditional liberalism, but democracy itself.

There is something to this meme, as we will see, and progressives would be wise, both philosophically and politically, to grapple with it. But memes—ideas that replicate rapidly in fertile cultural environments—are also worth questioning. That's because they tend to replicate without much conscious reflection on the part of those aiding in the replication. The need for reflection in this case is illustrated by one simple fact: those criticizing identity politics often don't really say what it is, or if they do, they conflate one meaning of the term with another.

Let's start by thinking briefly about what we mean by "identity" in this context. As we saw in Chapter 3, we can mean different things by that term too. We might mean our personal identity—that is, what makes us one and the same individual person *over time*. Or we might mean our self-identity, the kind of person we want to be. But when people talk about their identity politics, they are thinking primarily of their *social identity*: the social groups they belong to, including family, ethnicity, race, gender, sexual preference, and the roles they play in their social life.

At least two conceptions of the term "identity politics" are in use today in popular culture. The first use has its origins in philosophical concepts inherited from the Enlightenment but adapted for contemporary pluralist democracies. In this use, identity politics centers on advocating for public recognition of the concerns, needs, and rights of groups and identities that are often overlooked or marginalized in a society. In this use of the term, many forms of social activism and civil rights movements are exercises in identity politics.

The second use of the term is in many ways parasitic on the first. But it also names an arguably older idea: that politics is really just tribal warfare by other means. Identity politics, in this view, is standing up for your tribe—that is, the group you identify with—because it is your tribe. As we will see, this is an idea that is predicated on a particular view of what politics is for.

The problem with the "identity politics is bad" meme shooting around the internet today is that many people, including its critics and some advocates, tend to mush these two meanings together without realizing it. Observers on both sides of the aisle confuse those advocating for identity politics of the first kind with those advocating for identity politics of the second kind—and vice versa. That's a problem, not only because it leads people to talk past one another but because it has a tendency to obscure legitimate criticisms of either kind of identity politics. But more than that, and like other linguistic conflations we've seen in this book, it can be deliberately manipulated, making us think we know more than we do.

The current conflation of these two meanings of "identity politics" arguably stems from competing interpretations of one of the first contemporary uses of the term, in the 1977 political manifesto by the Combahee River Collective, a group of black feminist scholars that included the poet Audre Lorde and the writer and publisher Barbara Smith. In perhaps the mostly widely cited passage from the collective's statement, the group argued that civil rights, black power, and feminist movements had failed to adequately represent them. "We realize that the only people who care enough about us to work consistently for our liberation is us. . . . This focusing on our own oppression is embodied in the concept of identity politics. We believe that the most profound and potentially most radical politics come directly out of our own identity, as opposed to working to end somebody else's oppression."[4]

Mark Lilla, in his recent polemic against identity politics from the Left, takes this statement, with its concern for "our own identity" as indicative of what he considers the selfish nature of identity politics, according to which the most important politics are those that are meaningful to the self, and "the movements most meaningful to the self are, unsurprisingly, about the self."[5] Thus, according to Lilla, the Combahee River Collective, while advocating a kind of politics that is in part a "very good thing" (because it has encouraged people to focus on aspects of history that have long been ignored) has also encouraged a destructive individualism that undermines and devalues the idea of the common good—an idea that earlier Leftist movements, like Marxism, took for granted.

Lilla's reading of the collective's statement illustrates the second use of "identity politics" that I noted earlier. For Lilla, identity politics is overly focused on the self because it is focused on what I've called our self-identities—in particular those aspects connected to the groups we identify with. But more than that, he sees identity politics as incorporating a particular view about what politics is for: to advocate for power for one's group, national identity, or tribe and only for that group/identity/tribe. Many critics on the Right share this same conception of identity politics. Jonah Goldberg, in his recent book *Suicide of the West*, for example, argues that identity politics is only about power, and the use of it "to enthrone liberal ideals is inseparable from a desire for power— power for professors, students, activist groups, Democrats, etc."[6]

The idea that politics is all about power and tribe versus tribe is a sadly common one. It is also a dark vision, one that shares Machiavelli's view that politics is essentially war by other means. In the twentieth century, the most influential philosophical proponent of this idea was the infamous Nazi political theorist Carl Schmitt. Schmitt, who joined the Nazi Party in 1933, was active in book burnings of Jewish authors, openly advocated anti-Semitic policies, and remained unrepentant after the war. But he was also an influential political thinker, whose work remains important (and controversial).

Schmitt's most famous contribution concerned the purpose of politics. He argued that "the political is the most intense and extreme antagonism, and every concrete antagonism becomes that much more political the closer it approaches the most extreme point, that of the friend-enemy grouping."[7] For Schmitt, the idea of an enemy—a group of "others" to be opposed—is at the heart of politics itself. What Lilla and Goldberg agree on is that this conception of what politics is about underlies identity politics. Since they both want to reject Schmitt's dark vision, they both reject identity politics.

Lilla and Goldberg are right to reject the tribalist view of politics. It is also correct to say that some on the Left and the Right explicitly accept this sort of view, and there have always been philosophers who have argued its virtues. But I don't think many people who see themselves as explicitly practicing identity politics accept it, and for the simple reason already noted: *there is another way of understanding what "identity politics" means that doesn't imply an endorsement of the politics of tribalism.* Indeed, it is a clear misreading of the Combahee River Collective's statement to think they were endorsing the tribalist reading of the term they arguably introduced. Later in the same statement, the collective argues that "if Black women were free, it would mean that everyone would have to be free since our freedom would necessitate the destruction of all systems of oppression."[8] In other words, their focus on their own identity was practical: being black and a woman puts you at the center of a Venn diagram of sorts—one where the intersecting circles represent "women," "black," and "economically disadvantaged." The idea is that advocating for black women means engaging in a struggle for the freedom of people in all these circles. This is what is meant by "intersectionality."

This other view of identity politics starts from two premises. First, individuals have social identities, and it is an obligation of democracies to treat those social identities, as much as possible and within the constraints of other democratic values, with equal respect. Second, in contemporary democracies certain social identities are typically less privileged than others, and one way to be less privileged is for your identity—as black, a woman, gay, trans—to not even be recognized as *an* identity. That's why many social movements start by advocating for public recognition. It is why, for example, trans activists have argued that being trans is a normal way of being a human being, and that trans people (or gay men or lesbians) are not simply "sick."

Taken in this way, identity politics *just is* the politics of recognition. But recognition politics, unlike the politics of tribalism, implies no particular view of what politics is for. One might engage in politics in order to gain recognition for a social group for any number of reasons—to further that group's standing, to prevent it from being oppressed, or for the common good. One might, for example, argue that everyone is better off, when each of our social identities is recognized under the law. But independently of one's view on the point of politics, the justification for the importance of recognition in democratic theory is connected to the concept of equal respect—the first premise just mentioned. But why believe this premise?

The concept of equal respect has been a central component of democratic theory since Kant. The familiar idea is that each person should be treated equally under the law. The key is what that means, not just in terms of the notoriously difficult idea of "equality" but in terms of the concept of a person and identity itself.

In Chapter 3 I argued that one aspect of our overall identity— of what it means to be an individual, in other words—is that we each have a "self-identity," which is the kind of person we aspire to be, including our aspirational social identities or the groups we identify with. If so, then it is wrong to think of our identities atomistically, as if each person were a geometric point separated on a line from all others. Rather, our self-identities are constructed in relation to, and possibly in rebellion against, the social identities we inherit from the culture around us. Crucially, our identities are narratives written by us and others at the same time—partly through the process of recognition. My recognizing you (or not doing so) as being the kind of person you are helps to shape you—whether you like it or not—into being a particular kind of person. Social recognition is part of individual identity formation from the get-go. And so, if democracies wish to treat individuals with equal respect, they cannot help but recognize individuals as falling into certain categories. The formation of our self-identities requires such categorization.

Of course, antidemocratic societies aren't concerned with equal respect, even if they are concerned with recognition (being recognized as a lord or lady, for example). Only with the collapse of social hierarchies, together with the rising importance of human rights and the idea of basic respect, did the concepts of recognition and identity even become salient. But once they did, the fact that our self-identities are formed partly through social recognition also became politically salient. As a result, the social formation of our self-identities, together with the demands of respect and dignity, provides a reason for wanting one's identity recognized not just by other individuals but under the law.[9]

Even if this argument is accepted, there are complications when it comes to real—as opposed to theoretical—politics. Which identities should be recognized, and what counts as legal and political recognition, are issues that continue to animate real-world political discussions about gender, race, and religion. But those are not the issues that interest me here. My point so far is simpler: the politics of recognition is not the same as the politics of tribalism. The former is deeply linked to basic democratic ideals. The latter most assuredly is not.

It is therefore interesting that critics of identity politics often confuse those practicing the recognition version of identity politics with those practicing the tribal version. A good example is the reaction to Black Lives Matter—another group, like the Combahee River Collective, started by black women. The furor over the Black Lives Matter movement started with the hashtag and slogan itself. Many white people—both on the Left and on the Right—seemed to think it meant "*only* black lives matter." But as the creators of the movement pointed out right from the beginning, it meant "black lives matter *too*." The point of the movement was not to promote one race over the other, but to get whites to recognize that black citizens were disproportionately victims of police violence. The persistence of the misunderstanding was so prevalent that it was hard not to see it, at times, as deliberate.

If the distinction between these two ways of conceiving of identity politics is so obvious—as I've essentially just said it is—then why the confusion? Why do so many take recognition politics to be the politics of tribalism?[10]

One explanation, perhaps best made by the influential feminist and Marxist theorist Nancy Fraser, is that the politics of recognition often leads to damaging—that is, tribal—forms of "communitarianism." The thought is that concentrating one's political efforts on recognizing one's social identity can only underline the distinctiveness of one's community and serve to enforce that community's norms—norms that themselves, in the case of traditional communities, might not be egalitarian or progressive.[11] In short, Fraser worries that overemphasizing recognition can lead to underemphasizing issues of justice. That may be so, but as Fraser's critics have pointed out, one might argue that in many cases, certain social groups often need recognition *before* they can lobby for more just policies.[12] One precedes the other.

A different worry about recognition politics is that it can lead to a tribal view of knowledge. In part, this is because recognition politics is often associated with "standpoint epistemology"—a view about social knowledge that, like "identity politics," is often misunderstood. As developed by early feminist philosophers in the 1980s and '90s, standpoint epistemology rests on the intuitive thought that where you sit in society can give you insights that others often lack.[13] Seen in this way, it is an extension of a very old philosophical idea: experience matters. As the seventeenth-century empiricist John Locke put it, someone who tastes a pineapple for the first time (an exotic fruit in Locke's England) knows something that those who haven't had the pleasure don't know: what a pineapple tastes like. Similarly, pregnancy is an experience that gives a woman access to certain truths about her body, and about medical care, and social and personal relationships. Experiences like being pregnant or having children are "transformative": they change not only what you care about, but what kinds of knowledge you may have.[14]

Standpoint epistemologists applied this idea to the social realm: because of how they are treated in the general culture, because of how they are harassed by men, or denied certain privileges, women have insights into that culture that men don't have. The point can be generalized even further. A person who has experienced oppression (for whatever reason) has experiences that someone who has never been oppressed in that way doesn't have. And that experience can give them knowledge that others might have a hard time appreciating. Indeed, this was part of the point of the Combahee River Collective's statement.

A good example of how this theory interacts with recognition politics is the growing sensitivity to sexual harassment. Activists and ordinary citizens have used verbal and video testimony to bring public recognition to facts about what it is like to be a woman in this society that have often been overlooked or downplayed. The #MeToo movement has made people—or should we say, *men*—publicly accept that sexual violence and harassment is deeply widespread and tolerated in our society, particularly when it involves men with financial or political power over women. In doing so, activists have brought to light truths that previously had been appreciated from only a particular standpoint. They've brought recognition to knowledge that had been hidden.

Note that none of this requires or even encourages tribal politics. In fact, quite the opposite: it takes public recognition of certain identities as a step toward public, shared knowledge. Of course, that shared knowledge may be limited. I may know *that* racism and sexism exist without knowing what it is like to experience them. But I don't need to know what experiencing oppression (or starvation or rape) *is like* to be able to know that *it is bad*, and to vote accordingly.

A move toward tribalism happens only when one goes a step further and takes knowledge, and perhaps truth itself, as relative to certain standpoints. This is a step that many standpoint epistemologists have often been reluctant to take, but that many others sometimes do in their name. This was especially true in the 1980s and '90s, when identity politics and standpoint theory were often identified with postmodernism. A central insight of many forms of postmodernism is the idea that categories that Western culture often treated as natural and given—like race or gender or even identity itself—are to varying degrees actually social constructions.

A social construction is not a literal artifact, like a chair or a hammer. Where hammers are defined by their functions, social constructions are defined by social practices. Some of these practices are totally unregulated. Being cool, for example, is the product of social expectations, but not expectations that are encoded in law or custom per se. The laws of the cool change rapidly from generation to generation, and in ways that the older generation will rarely predict or even understand. But other social constructions—like marriage—*are* a matter of meeting certain regulated conditions, in this case legal regulations. One can't be married unless one meets those conditions. And the same can be said for much of what we take for granted in our social world—wealth, religion, laws, and government. You can't define such things without appealing to certain structured forms of human behavior and thinking.[15]

The idea that much of our life is determined by social constructions is a powerful philosophical insight. Even more important is the insight that we often confuse a category like race or marriage as naming a natural kind of thing as opposed to something that has been socially constructed. But both of these ideas are different still from the idea that *truth itself* is constructed. According to that view, the truth of what we say or believe is determined not by how things "really are" but by our social practices. Truth, as the philosopher Richard Rorty once ironically suggested, is what your peers let you get away with saying.[16]

This kind of relativism about truth is sometimes associated with identity politics and progressivism in general. Those convinced by the association—on the Left and on the Right—often seem to make an inference like this: (1) our standpoints are social constructions; (2) our standpoints determine what we think is true; hence, (3) truth is relative to standpoints.

This can be a seductive argument. Part of its power lies in the fact that its premises are plausible. My social standpoint *is* largely the result of culture. And my opinions *are* generally a result of that standpoint—of the collection of social identities and perspectives that make it up. But an even greater part of the argument's seductive power is the egalitarian appeal of its conclusion. For, the idea that what is true is determined by where I socially stand can seem like a great leveling device, suggesting that every standpoint is as good as any other from the point of view of knowledge. No one has the God's-eye point of view, so no one should be tempted to claim it. For this reason, perhaps more than any other, many progressives—for whom equality is a supreme value—have been tempted by an idea that seems to make all truths equal.

But it is fallacious to infer truth relativism from those premises. The fact that what I *think* is true depends on my perspective doesn't make the truth itself relative to that perspective. That would be like thinking that just because I can see the next valley only from the top of the ridge means that the next valley exists only when I stand there. Moreover, the idea that truth is relative in this way is deeply implausible. It suggests that thinking you are bulletproof (and getting everyone else to believe it too) would mean you really are bulletproof. The fact that all thinking is done from a perspective doesn't mean that thinking makes it so. In particular, race and gender are social constructions, but that doesn't mean that *that very fact* (the fact that race and gender are social constructions) is a social construction.

Truth relativism, however, *is* an idea that can lead to a form of tribal politics, and, as we saw in Chapter 4, it can support an ideology of arrogance. These outcomes can sound surprising, since, as I just noted, many liberals and progressives have embraced forms of relativism about truth and knowledge precisely because they seemed to promise the ultimate kind of equality: equality of belief. And this was meant to lead to tolerance. (Conservative thinkers like Bill Bennett and Alan Bloom reinforced the connection between equality and tolerance during the 1980s and '90s, arguing that the idea that all beliefs could be true was the scourge of the Earth, and denouncing liberals for espousing it.)

The number of people who actually embrace relativism is hard to determine. The question is partly one of language. I've noticed over the years that "truth is relative" or "that's true for me" can mean lots of different things to different people—from "I have my opinion, you have yours, so let's go have a beer" to a commonsense skepticism about the difficulty of knowing what is really true. But taken seriously as a philosophical view, relativism encourages less tolerance and more tribalism than one might have thought.

Here's why. According to relativism, for any proposition P, P is true at some time if, and only if, my perspective sanctions P at that time. It follows that whatever my perspective sanctions can't be false, because those propositions are, *by definition, true*. And the same is the case relative to your perspective. Thus, where your perspective sanctions a proposition and mine does not, we both believe what is true and neither of us is mistaken.

But how, then, can we settle our disagreements? Not by appealing to common facts, because truth is relative to perspectives. So, where my standpoint differs from yours, so does my truth. As such, a rational solution to our disagreement—one based on the facts—seems out of reach. And that unattainability can lead to the dark thought that the only way to resolve our dispute is for me to get you to share my perspective or recognize it as the privileged one. Then my truth will be all the truth there is; there will be no speaking truth to power.

Note that this form of tribalism bites its own tail, for the same logic means, in turn, that I can't even criticize my own current perspective. What is true at some time, in such a view, is what is sanctioned by the perspective at that time. So, whatever my perspective sanctions at some moment in time is never wrong at that moment in time. Which, in turn, means that we can never describe my perspective as progressing, since to progress is to improve from moment to moment. But if what is true is true relative to a perspective in a particular moment, then my perspective never improves from moment to moment. It only changes. This is the dark place—the denial of the possibility of moral and social progress—toward which truth relativism leads.

There is no doubt that much of the Left for a very long time fell victim to these sorts of ideas. But nothing in recognition politics or standpoint epistemology, or even the idea of social construction *requires* truth relativism. As Sandra Harding herself—arguably the central figure in standpoint epistemology—argued forcefully way back in 1993:

> It is not equally true as its denial that women's uteruses wander around in their bodies when they take math courses, that only Man the Hunter made important contributions to society . . . that targets of rape and battery must bear the responsibility for what happens to them. . . . Standpoint theories neither hold nor are doomed to hold [relativism about truth].[17]

So, identifying identity politics—and associated epistemological theories like standpoint theory—with relativism is simply a mistake, but it is a mistake that the Left has paid dearly for making. One cost is the arrogance of belief that it has inspired, an arrogance that encourages some progressives to feel that because their truth is their truth, they—and the social groups for which they believe they stand—have nothing to learn from conservatives, or anyone else for that matter. That's the sort of arrogant ideology that leads progressives to turn their nose up at even talking to Trump voters, or makes some college students unwilling to debate with conservative intellectuals when they come to their campus.

Another cost of linking identity politics with relativism is that it has inspired imitators on the Right—perhaps best epitomized by the Trump administration's penchant for talking about "alternative facts." And there is no getting around the fact that the current and frightening resurgence of the Alt-Right is due to a renewed commitment to tribal politics on the Right. Indeed, in the United States the *ur-tribal politics has always been the politics of white supremacy*, which pits tribe against tribe in the most explicit way possible, and which brooks no truth other than its own dark light.

It is a confusion to blame identity politics for intellectual arrogance on the Left. More to blame is the relativism about truth and knowledge that is sometimes associated with such politics—even though it is not essential to them.

The Rationality Brand

One of Conservapedia's chief examples of liberal arrogance is the 2016 election, about which it says, "Virtually the entire liberal media arrogantly proclaimed that the election of Hillary Clinton was 'inevitable' and a 'foregone conclusion.'"[18]

This claim is fair enough, but it was not just the liberal media that made this mistake. It was liberals themselves. A common idea, especially during the spring of 2016, that was passed around at progressives' dinner parties was that the country could not be so "dumb/racist/sexist/____" as to elect Donald Trump. He could not be taken seriously. He was an obvious huckster, a fraud and a liar, more an object of ridicule than a serious political opponent. The one to fear, many thought, was Ted Cruz. Or even Marco Rubio. But not Trump. Many of my friends, moreover, thought that the arc of history, not to mention demographics, was bending toward the Democrats. It was time for a woman president and Democrats had the female candidate, while Republicans had backed the most openly misogynist candidate ever to run for office.

Many liberals only started to doubt this narrative very late in the game. One troubling sign was a minor kerfuffle the week before the election over statistician Nate Silver's predictions for the presidential race. At the time, HuffPost and other media sites were predicting well over a 90 percent chance of victory for Clinton. But right before the election, Silver lowered his prediction to 65 percent, alarming many on the Left. After all, this was the man who had successfully predicted that Barack Obama would win in 2012 (over Republican pollsters who had been forecasting a confident victory for the Right). Snarling that Silver was "putting his thumb on the scales," HuffPost loudly denounced his tactics.[19] Silver just as loudly defended them, pointing out that he was simply trying to adjust for the possibility that many of the polls were making some background assumptions that might just turn out to be wrong. It all got rather nasty on social media, and I remember thinking that if we liberals were really so confident (after all, Silvers was still predicting that Trump had only a 35 percent chance!), then why were we so set on the idea not just that Trump would lose, but that *we all had to agree that it was almost certain Trump would lose*?

In retrospect, this was a sign that intellectual arrogance was indeed at work on the Left during that election. For many on the Left, a self-defensive concern for our tribe's collective self-esteem was more important for what they believed than was the truth itself. We were living in bad faith.

After the election, this realization caused a paroxysm of collective self-doubt, anger, shock, and disbelief—all of which are pretty common when a political party loses an election. At the university where I work in New England, some professors canceled classes, some students didn't get out of bed, and talk about needing counseling shot up. Fox News had a field day. Trump's victory seemingly vindicated its viewership's position that universities are riddled with liberals and snowflakes. And it was consistent with the thought that for many Trump voters, the most important thing wasn't policy, but seeing arrogant liberals (and the party of a black president) getting their comeuppance.

This conservative attitude betrays its own kind of arrogance. But I also think there is no avoiding the fact that conservatives are reacting to something that is real and present in the way that many liberals see the world and that encompasses the liberal ideology of arrogance. We might gloss that something as "liberals know best." We are in command of the facts; they aren't. We are rational and scientific; they aren't. We are compassionate; they aren't. We are not racist or sexist; they are.

These are the sorts of assumptions that lead so many on the Left to often act as if all conservatives must be not just mistaken in their values but dumb (because they don't know the facts) and/or duped (because they've been tricked into ignoring the facts). In other words, liberal Democrats tend to think of themselves as the "knowing" party, bound by its common knowledge of the real facts: "*Knowing*, for example, that the Founding Fathers were all secular deists. *Knowing* that you're actually, like, 30 times more likely to shoot yourself than an intruder. *Knowing* that those fools out in Kansas are voting against their own self-interest and that the trouble is Kansas doesn't know any better. *Knowing* all the jokes that signal this knowledge."[20]

One can quarrel with these examples. And it would be wrong to assume that liberals are more prone to groupthink than conservatives. There is more than enough of that to go around on all sides. What is important is that widespread unquestioned assumptions are all the more problematic *when anti-groupthink is part of your self-conscious brand*. And it is hard to argue with the idea that being the party of "critical thinking" is part of liberals' own conception of themselves. Liberals represent the politics of knowledge and reason; conservatives represent the politics of emotion and blind faith.

This (mis)identification is rooted in two debates that, while distinct, are often conflated. The older of the two is philosophical. It concerns the role that traditional liberal *political philosophy* suggests that reason plays in political justification. That view is long-standing and predates current political divisions. It stems, in part, from attempts by philosophers as different as Rousseau, Locke, and Kant to ground democratic politics in reason and experience—an attempt that saw its apex in the twentieth-century philosophical work of Jürgen Habermas and John Rawls. The thought, very broadly speaking, is that legitimate democratic policies, at least in the ideal, would result from free and reasoned agreement between equal citizens. Democratic governments didn't enforce their will by appeal to either divine right, custom, or social tradition alone.

Old-school liberal theory's reliance on ideals of rationality to ground democracy has long been a target of conservative intellectuals from Edmund Burke onward. Michael Oakeshott, for example, a philosophical hero of traditional conservatism in the United States and Britain, influentially argued during the mid-twentieth century that liberal political philosophy is a kind of rationalism, and that this rationalism, and its consequent spurning of traditional community norms, is its undoing. The liberal, Oakeshott argued, saw himself as "the enemy of authority, of prejudice, of the merely traditional, customary or habitual. His mental attitude is at once skeptical and optimistic. . . . Moreover he is fortified by a belief in 'reason' common to all mankind."[21]

Oakeshott saw the liberal attitude as dangerously naïve. The problem was its implicit assumption that, in rising above tradition, it can rise above prejudice and bias. But, Oakeshott argued, this it could not do, because knowledge is always formed in the context of a tradition, a custom, a way of life. His reasoning anticipated similar criticism of traditional liberalism later made from the Right by writers such as Roger Scruton and David Brooks, and from the Left by Richard Rorty, Judith Butler, Charles Mills, and others. Traditional liberal philosophy portrayed itself as immune from bias, these critics warned, but that attitude only served to hide its own prejudices from itself. It perpetuates a form of bad faith and, therefore, a kind of intellectual arrogance.

This is an important criticism, although I still believe that the giving of and asking for reasons is a central stone in democracy's foundation. Moreover, we can defend reasons, and certain aspects of liberal political philosophy, without defending the idea that human beings are Reasoners with a capital R—that we are unembodied logical inference machines. We might say that reasons matter for democracy, but Reason, not so much.[22]

Whatever the outcome of this first philosophical debate— concerning the foundations of democracy—it is different from another, more explicitly political debate that is sometimes confused with it. This second debate is about whether liberal progressivism is somehow tied to intellectual elitism. This debate is more mainstream—and is often distorted by those on both the Left and the Right.

One way that concerns over intellectual elitism show up is in shifts in attitudes toward higher education. Consider, for example, the growing suspicion of universities by many on the Right. The Pew Research Center reported in 2017 that 58 percent of Republicans and Republican-leaning independents say that institutions of higher education have a negative effect on the way things are going in the country, while just 36 percent say that their effect is positive. That number is, frankly, astounding. It is astounding not only because even Republicans who acknowledge they have benefited financially from college feel that way but because, just two years ago, *attitudes were actually flipped*: a 54 percent majority of Republicans and Republican leaners said that universities were having a positive effect, while 37 percent said their effect was negative.[23] In other words, in the span of just two years most Republicans have gone from thinking institutions of higher education are helping the country to thinking they're hurting it.

And it seems pretty clear that the harm that conservatives think universities are imposing on the country isn't financial; it's cultural. An old college friend of mine—very liberal when young but more conservative now—confided to me that he was, in fact, deeply worried about higher education, even as he saved to send his kids to the best schools. He worried because "it seems like no one has an open mind anymore. Students just want to shout people down." He had in mind "no-platforming" protests against conservative campus speakers, or incidents, such as one at my own university, in which student activists put a halt to a conservative provocateur defending the idea that "it is okay to be white." (Which seems, frankly, like getting up to defend the idea that it is okay to like ice cream. No one really has been worrying about it, have they?) That these incidents are markedly different is worth pointing out: just a few years ago students were protesting nerdy Harvard professors; now they are protesting active white supremacists. Nonetheless, my friend had a point, and one that many progressive faculty members worry about too, if only because pushing antidemocratic ideas underground doesn't make them go away.

In any event, the idea that universities are bastions of liberalism is neither new nor surprising, largely because it is true. A number of studies over the last decade, some quite recent, have supported the basic perception held by most students and faculty themselves: that faculty at universities and colleges lean largely left. In New England, liberal faculty members have been found to outnumber conservatives twenty-eight to one.[24] Critics on both the Right and the Left (for example, Jonah Goldberg and Nicholas Kristof) often portray the humanities and social sciences as ground zero for this disparity—where, according to these views, fields are run largely by professors of ethnic and gender studies.[25]

But while it is true that many historians, sociologists, and philosophers, for example, have led the way in theorizing about identity, it isn't clear that such fields are more dominated by liberal-leaning academics than are the sciences. Indeed, the data points in the other direction. Even in 2009, according to Pew, only 6 percent of scientists working in the United States identified as Republicans.[26] This suggests that your average neighborhood physicist, just like your neighborhood philosopher, is far more likely than the average American to be liberal and not particularly religious, and to give to Democratic politicians over Republicans.

Since liberal dominance of academe is not new, the amazing uptick in negative attitudes toward colleges and universities among conservatives can't be credited simply to conservatives' sudden discovery that liberals are teaching their kids ("I'm shocked—*shocked*—to find liberalism going on in this establishment!"). Instead, this rising negativity seems more likely to be the result of other factors, including both an increase in the attention of media like Fox News and the upswing of anti-elite rhetoric in the Trump era. Looked at through this newly dominant frame, the academy represents the clearest case—even more so than Hollywood, another conservative target—of the idea that "intellectual elites" are both politically out of line with the rest of the country and arrogant know-it-alls that look down on the hardworking average American.

But it is far from clear that liberal dominance has had the effects that its detractors fear, since most students, liberal or conservative, seem to go through college without changing their political views.[27] The real issue with liberal dominance of higher education, then, is not its immediate practical effects. It is not leading to the great social change hoped for by progressives or feared by conservatives. The real issue is not what liberal dominance of higher education is doing to our culture, but what the political conditions surrounding the discussion about it is doing to progressive liberalism.

The basic problem is a kind of negative feedback loop. Conservative accusations of elitism can cause defensive reactions that, perversely, can encourage that very elitism. One reason for this is that accusations of elitism can cause liberal status-threat anxiety. (And perhaps reasonably so: it is reasonable to worry about those who think you are corrupting the minds of the youth.) But status-threat anxiety, as I argued earlier, whether in response to a real threat or a perceived one, can itself feed arrogance. Think of it this way: if you are forced to defend why there are so few conservatives in the academy, it is very tempting to conclude the reason is that they tried but failed (or would have failed had they tried). In other words, the worry is not liberal dominance in the academy, but the fact that in the current social conditions, liberal thinking can play into our very human *tendency to believe our own hype*, which means accepting that progressive liberalism alone can be the standard-bearer for reason.[28]

Here's another way to describe the worry. Earlier I noted that there is a long-standing philosophical debate about whether we can justify our political arrangements by reason and experience alone (the traditional liberal view) or whether we also need to appeal to custom and tradition (the traditional conservative view). But that philosophical question has been almost entirely replaced by a different one: whether contemporary progressive liberals (*the people, not the theory*) are more rational—whether they are smarter than conservatives, *just by virtue of being liberal.* This new question is troubling for all sorts of reasons. The self-conception that one's tribe just knows more, *whether or not it is correct,* can lead, if we are not careful, to confusing a commitment to truth with a commitment to one's own superiority. That is a hallmark of the kind of bad faith that I've argued is part and parcel of intellectual arrogance. And this is exactly the sort of arrogance that can also lead to not taking the opposition seriously enough, to underestimating them, and to confusing ridicule with effective opposition. It's the sort of bad faith that can lead to the election of authoritarian despots.

The Politics of Contempt

It is very possible that as you've been reading this book, you have been alternating between two different feelings. One is a feeling of recognition: you've thought something along the lines of "Yeah, their arrogance really is dangerous!" The other is indignation: "We're not being arrogant (in doing X). We're just being reasonable!" This back-and-forth feeling is understandable, but if I'm right, it is also a symptom of the problem.

Not long ago I was at a barbecue at the house of a well-known scientist at an Ivy League university. We had just returned from attending a workshop on political polarization together. As we stood beside the grill, drinking beer, he turned to me and remarked, "You know, as much as I admire open-mindedness and civility and all that, I can't help feeling that right now is not the time. Screw them." He was talking, of course, about politics, and Trumpian conservatives in particular.

The anger that my colleague was giving voice to is probably familiar to all of us. I know I often feel it; it is hard not to, it seems, in contemporary America, and not just on the Left. It has been something of a mantra for many hard-line conservatives for some time, as even the most casual listener of hard-Right radio programs, or reader of Alt-Right blogs, well knows.

A telling example is the case of the Listen First Project. Founded by moderately conservative, Christian graduate student Pearce Godwin, it aims to encourage people to "listen first and vote second." Its mission is noble: to encourage productive dialogue nationwide. But Listen First became tremendously controversial when it held its first national meeting (with numerous high-level speakers) in Charlottesville, Virginia, the locale a year earlier of a violent protest by white supremacists that had ended in the murder of a counterdemonstrator. Many local activists took Godwin's call to listen as directed at them, and they saw it as code for "sit down and shut up." Godwin protested that this was not his intention, yet for many people, the call to "listen first" in Charlottesville was deeply offensive. Many of the racists marching in Charlottesville were self-described Nazis who had chanted, "Jews will not replace us." Who wants to listen first to Nazis? Screw them.

The misgivings about attempts to dialogue extend beyond

just wanting not to hear vile chants. The worry is that sometimes being tolerant of intolerance can encourage it. Joseph Goebbels, Nazi minister of propaganda for the Third Reich, famously said that the greatest joke on democracy was that it gave its enemies the means by which it could be destroyed. By this he meant that democratic freedoms could be used to undermine those same freedoms, to turn people against them.

As Jason Stanley has emphasized, it is not difficult to see that this same tactic is at work right now by the Alt-Right Nazis of the day. The white supremacists marching in Charlottesville were using democratic protections of free speech and assembly to endorse deeply antidemocratic views—views according to which nonwhites should (literally) be second-class citizens. And the same tactics, one might argue, can be seen on the pages of Breitbart and tumbling out of the president's Twitter rants. Some conspiracy theorists repeatedly endorsed the idea that the murder of schoolchildren at Sandy Hook Elementary School was a politically motivated hoax and argued that they were just "acting as reporters" and "investigating the truth." One can't object to *that*, right? Well, actually one can, unless one thinks that looking things up on 4chan and inventing things out of whole cloth amounts to journalism. Such conspiracy theorists are using democratic means (free speech protections) to undermine democracy.

Another reason we can feel resistant to calls for democratic dialogue is that we are as divided over what counts as "democratic" as we are over anything else. That's nothing new in democracies, where dissent and disagreement is part of the point, and where the very meaning of core values is always up for renegotiation. But it is particularly salient now. Donald Trump infamously declared that some of those who marched on Charlottesville were "fine people"—by which he presumably meant (in a supercharitable reading) that some white protesters might have been motivated out of something other than pure racism and they should be allowed to express themselves. Yet apparently, he also thinks that (mostly) black football players kneeling during the national anthem should not be allowed that same self-expression, that they are "traitors." And Trump, presumably, is not alone in these sentiments.

There is a third complicating factor motivating feelings of anger in politics. Calls to civility and dialogue can themselves be divisive partly because they legitimately mean different things, depending on where you sit. The key variable is power. As any negotiator or moderator can tell you, dialogue feels different when you hold more cards than when you hold fewer, if only because the outcome of any exchange is more likely to be in your favor.

For all these reasons, some reading these pages may find my concerns with intellectual arrogance worrisome. When you are feeling outrage, calls to being open to your own fallibility can sound like a request to waver in your convictions. You don't feel fallible when you are angry. You feel right. And anger can be a useful political emotion; it motivates and focuses. But anger is also a gateway to a more complicated moral emotion: contempt.

Try this thought experiment: Imagine you had a drug that could cause people to believe in your political point of view. What would you do with it? Give it to your racist uncle? Send it to your local congressional representative? Drop it in the water supply?

You would be tempted. After all, politics is a high-stakes game, and getting people to believe "the truth" would save lives. But I've also found that even for people who would be willing to drop the drug into the water supply, most agree that there is something clearly wrong with doing so. Why? Because you aren't asking people their opinions; you aren't treating them as capable of making up their own minds. Dropping the political correctness drug into the water without people's knowledge is a clear violation of what we might call basic respect.

As we saw earlier, one of the most fundamental demo-cratic ideals—an ideal that lies behind one conception of iden-tity politics—is that that we owe each other basic respect. In a democracy, those in power can't simply enforce their will without justification, because doing so violates that respect. Likewise, it is wrong to win our political battles by manipulation and deceit. That's partly why fake news stories that spread online for politi-cal purposes rankle us. We are being used; being treated as mere dupes; being treated, as Kant would have put it, "as a mere means" to other ends, not as ends ourselves.

This connection between respect and democracy is why we think that citizens are accountable to one another. No matter how different we may be individually, under the law we are all equal. And democracy is partly grounded on this fact. By trading in real reasons rather than "fake news" (or in brainwashing drugs as in the thought experiment I proposed earlier), we acknowledge that we owe each other some basic respect, and not just legally but as cognitive agents, *as knowers and believers*. Treating people with this kind of respect doesn't mean you treat everyone as an expert. That would be silly. But it does mean treating people not only as capable of making up their own minds but as possible sources of knowledge.

The mansplainer who repackages a woman's point and explains it back to her (as his own insight, naturally) is, for this reason, showing a lack of basic respect. When men do this, they aren't discounting their conversational partners because they think their partners are less informed but because they see their partners' contributions as fundamentally less important than their own. They are taking those contributions to be less credible. And in so doing, they implicitly signal that they don't feel they have to answer to a woman either. The sexist does not think of himself as accountable to women, and the general know-it-all doesn't think he is accountable to anyone but himself. That's an undemocratic attitude. In a democracy, at least in the ideal, we are accountable to one another.[29]

This is why it is dangerous to allow contempt to inform our approach to political *policy*. Like its hotter cousin anger, cold contempt feels good, and it is sometimes justified. But infused into policy, it can lead to something darker: that we should back policies—as opposed to individual attitudes—that treat those we oppose as undeserving of basic respect. There is no doubt that this is a choice that many feel pressed upon them: the choice of whether to resist the use of democratic means toward undemocratic ends by using undemocratic means for democratic ends. In other words, the choice, many feel, concerns whether to defend democracy by being undemocratic—that is, whether to take political steps that force our beliefs on others—to engage in the equivalent of dropping the drug into the water supply. Emotionally speaking, that's switching from respect to contempt.

The temptation to abandon basic respect in favor of contempt wouldn't be too concerning, if not for the fact that there is increasingly little in American life that is politics-free.[30] Where we live, the cars we drive, the food we eat, the schools and churches we attend, the hobbies and sports we enjoy, the books we read, the television shows we watch, the clothes we wear—these are all increasingly tribalized. Everything has become laden with meaning, and a deep meaning at that, and liberals' use of social media to shame and mock has certainly contributed to that fact.

As our discussions in earlier chapters suggested, when ordinary things and issues become laden with meaning, the realm of the political—*the realm of conviction*—expands. And when that happens, what was once a matter of debate or even dialogue can become a matter of power and an opportunity for disdain and moral contempt.

Contempt is a deeply complex, almost paradoxical emotion. It is how we treat someone who is beyond the pale, who has committed not just a moral failure but has failed *as a person*. To fail as a person, in the sense I mean here, is to be regarded as having forfeited respect. This is different from just being regarded as an ingrate, or as reckless, or as simply having false beliefs. The contemptible person is not just someone who has done a moral wrong. Stealing doesn't make someone contemptible just on that basis. To hold the thief in contempt for his act of thievery, we must know something more—or think we know something more—about him. We must see him as having known better, and at the same time regard him as having, to some measure, responsibility for an irredeemable character. The target of contempt, as opposed to someone who has managed to do something wrong, is regarded as inferior in some respect, as not worth the effort.

Like any emotion, contempt comes in degrees. To hold someone in extreme or total contempt, is to see him in two lights: first, as a moral failure *as a person*, and thus no longer deserving of the basic respect that persons enjoy, and second, as being responsible for this failing. To treat someone with total contempt is to act, incoherently, as though personhood is a test that one (that is, a person) can pass or fail. But this very assumption is what enables contempt to justify the most inhumane acts.

Contempt is a powerful attitude, but it is not a particularly democratic one.[31] And that is something that liberals would do well to heed. I say this because I, like everyone else nowadays, do have contempt for many of my political opponents. I, too, feel the rage of righteousness. But I also have come to recognize its danger. Once one feels contempt for someone or some ideology, respect disappears almost as a matter of definition. One does not work to compromise with those one holds in contempt. One does not seek an overlapping consensus with their values, or wish to have one's kids associate with them, or try to converse with them at a dinner party, or step in to aid them when they are threatened or bullied. That's the danger that liberals need to be mindful of. The twin of arrogance is contempt, but contempt is not the sort of attitude that is easy to come back from. Anger, even resentment, can come and go. But once you are contemptuous of something, it is hard to climb back out of that hole. That, however, is the hole we on the Left are digging for ourselves, even as we scorn those on the Right doing the same.

6

Truth and Humility
as Democratic Values

Socratic Lessons

One of the oldest methods for pursuing truth in the Western tradition is the elenchus—the Socratic method. In its basic form, it is an exchange between two people: one who questions and one who answers. In Socrates's own hands, it was often a relentless but frustrating march that ended not in a great reveal of truth but in an admission of ignorance. It usually involved questioning someone who imperiously claimed to know quite a bit about something important. It typically ended with the examinees either admitting that they knew less than they claimed or suddenly finding they had another appointment. This passage about knowledge, from the dialogue known as the *Theaetetus*, is representative:

Socrates: It is by wisdom the wise are wise?

Theaetetus: Yes.

Socrates: And is that different in any way from knowledge?

Theaetetus: What?

Socrates: Wisdom; are not men wise in that which they know?

Theaetetus: Certainly, they are.

Socrates: Then wisdom and knowledge are the same?

Theaetetus: Yes.

Socrates: So here lies the difficulty which I can never solve to my satisfaction—What is knowledge? Can we answer that question? What say you? Which of us will speak first? . . . Why is there no reply?[1]

The process, in short, often seemed rather painful. Socrates admitted as much himself during his later trial, where he reported what happened when he cross-examined a politician who was heralded as wise:

I tried to explain to him that he thought himself wise but was not really wise; and the consequence was that he hated me. . . . So I left him, saying to myself as I went away: Well, although I don't suppose that either of us know anything really beautiful and good, I am better off than he is—for he knows nothing, but thinks that he knows. I neither know nor think that I know.[2]

Socrates's remark here highlights two distinctive elements of his method, both of which are relevant to the central puzzle we've been concerned with in this book: how to go about believing and holding our convictions.

The first element concerns the people to whom that method was frequently addressed: the arrogant and the powerful. The greater your power, Socrates seems to say, the more you should be concerned about the manner in which you are forming your opinions, and the more you should be open to the possibility that you've confused ego with truth. Indeed, as Plato lays out in *The Republic*, Socrates was particularly keen to refute the most explicit version of this view. Voiced by the character Thrasymachus, it is the idea that "justice is in the interests of the stronger," or as we sometimes put it, "might makes right." That dark saying has always been seductive to the powerful, for obvious reasons. It is a philosophical apology for intellectual arrogance. And in combating it, Socrates faced, by way of his trial and eventual death sentence, the typical consequence that befalls those who question power.

The other element of the Socratic method that comes through in the passage just quoted is that Socrates's concern with intellectual arrogance began with himself. His starting point was his awareness of his own limitations, his awareness of what he didn't know. This is the starting point that so inspired Montaigne in his tower and formed the basis of the warning in his writings of the dangers of intellectual arrogance for politics.

In stressing that the path to true wisdom begins with realizing what you don't know, Socrates was not alone among the ancients, whether from Europe or Asia. Lao-tzu made the same point: "To know that you don't know is best. Not to know that you don't know is a flaw."[3] One can read both philosophers, moreover, as emphasizing more than just the simple acknowledgment of our limited knowledge. Both were concerned with pointing out that our lack of knowledge was often due to our biases, our presumptions, our obsessions, and our blind spots. Thus, Socrates stresses, the politicians were prone to confuse power with knowledge, the successful tended to think that knowledge in one area meant knowledge in all, and the rhetorician replaced truth with persuasion.

It is notoriously difficult to know exactly what Socrates's considered views actually were. Our best source on his philosophy—Plato—had his own agenda, both intellectually and politically. Aristophanes, in *The Clouds*, portrays Socrates as a nutty crank, an attacker of tradition who was concerned only with twisting people's words—with making them move like the statues of Daedalus, even when the speaker wanted them to remain still. The one thing everyone agrees on is that Socrates was a searching questioner, pestering everyone around him, friend or foe. During his trial in Athens for corrupting the minds of the youth, he noted that he would be comfortable with a sentence of death as long as he was able to question the spirits in Hades.

Whatever the faults of his method, Socrates teaches us some essential lessons pertaining to our question of how to believe. The lessons are the result of his most fundamental insight: that in trying to figure out what to believe, we should, as much as possible, subject our assumptions to critical examination. Only then can we pursue truth over ego and avoid the arrogance that so afflicts the powerful.

The first lesson we've just discussed, and it has been a constant theme of this book: to pursue the truth seriously, we must first own our own cognitive limitations.[4] We need to come to grips with the fact not only that we do not know everything but that much of what we think we know may be due to our prejudices and assumptions. We must realize that our convictions may be the result of the blind acceptance of larger cultural narratives, and not the result of principled reflection.

Unlike Montaigne, Socrates was no skeptic. He thought that humans should at least strive to know, and that the striving itself was crucial for politics. But he didn't see it as something you could do alone. Inquiry for Socrates was dialectical. Knowledge, if one were ever to gain it, would come from dialogue with others.

It is a sign of the digital landscape in which we live—a landscape dotted with humans bent over the black mirrors of their phones—that we need an ancient Greek philosopher to tell us to talk to one another. Human dialogue is still some of the best software we have for the pursuit of knowledge. Naturally, there are different ways to engage in it, depending on our aims. We may be aiming to win, to justify our points and show the other side the error of their ways. Or our aim may be to solve problems, to weigh the evidence, and to share information. Or we may seek to simply understand, to explore both our differences and our commonalities.[5] Which of these aims Socrates had in mind is a matter of debate, and I won't weigh in on that matter here. For our purposes, the more important point is that discussion with others can be beneficial from the standpoint of knowledge—even if neither side, as in the Socratic dialogues, reaches a settled opinion.

In other words, we can learn from talking to others even when we don't end up agreeing with them. For example, we might come to know at least what view *not* to hold, or we might simply learn that we don't know what to think. But there is a deeper point here that is often overlooked: in talking to others, we often learn what we believe ourselves.[6]

By this, I don't just mean that we can *discover* what we really think through talking things through. That's true, but the statement is also misleading. It assumes a picture of thought and language according to which our concepts, and hence our beliefs and convictions, are settled and precise. The metaphor suggests that through the process of dialogue we just uncover them, bring them out into the light. We just needed to find the right language, the right words, to express our already perfectly clear thoughts.

This, of course, can happen. But something else also happens: we sometimes don't discover but *create* convictions while in conversation with others, or while participating in public discourse. Most people do not have particularly precise or carefully thought-out moral and political beliefs. One reason for that is obvious: we don't have the time or inclination to think through all of the ramifications of difficult policies on taxes, immigration, trade, and so on, let alone plumb the depths of political thinkers like Plato or Adam Smith or Kant. People, after all, have things to do: families to raise, careers to pursue, art to create.

So, one reason our political views lack precision is that we lack the time to make them more precise. But another reason is endemic to those beliefs themselves: it is often that the very *concepts* we employ in politics—general concepts like fairness or liberty, as well as specific concepts like marriage or immigration—are themselves unsettled. Their boundaries are not precise; or they may have a core that can be stretched and made more precise in very different ways.

Many of our concepts—not just the political ones—are unsettled in this way. Wittgenstein pointed out that many of our concepts apply to things that have only a "family resemblance" to one another. The members of a family may not have any particular feature that they and only they share in common, but rather a set of overlapping features: some may share the same nose but not hair color, others may have the same hair color and height but different builds, and so on. Nonetheless, because of the crisscrossing nature of their characteristics, we can spot the resemblance.

Wittgenstein thought that games, too, only shared overlapping features: some games are competitive, but not all are (think of a child throwing a ball against a wall); others involve teams, but not all do; some have explicit rules, but others' rules change or are created on the spot. The concept of a game is thus unsettled or fluid; no single characteristic or essence nails down what a game can be. As a result, we are free to create new things that nonetheless we find useful to label as games because we can spot the resemblance. The same is true, Wittgenstein thought, with many of our concepts, and it is not difficult to see his point. Concepts as different as jazz, religion, and pornography all seem like this. They apply to things with not a single defining essence but an expanding family of characteristics.

Because of their fluid and unsettled nature, our disputes about what counts as a game or religion or jazz, for example, often take the form of an explicit negotiation. This is apparent to anyone who remembers negotiating the rules of a newly invented playground game, or has played with a child, or has engaged in barroom discussions about whether figure skating really should be counted as an Olympic sport. In such situations, we are aware that we are often simply trying to justify stretching the concept one way rather than another.[7]

My point is that many of the concepts we use in our political debates are like this.[8] Take the concept of marriage, for example. Political arguments about that concept were, for some time, focused on whether it could even apply to a union other than that between a man and a woman, with some people arguing that it could not, and others, victoriously as it turned out, arguing that it could. Advocates on both sides would sometimes act as if the concept were perfectly settled; it was just a matter of everyone recognizing where its precise boundaries lay. But I think it more likely that we were negotiating those boundaries during political discourse about the concept, engaging in an exchange of reasons both implicit and explicit for pulling the concept in one direction rather than another. Moreover, I don't think this case is atypical. Public discussion is often a continual process of conceptual renegotiation that is a combination of creation and discovery. It is a process that teaches us something; we not only learn from it how our concepts are used, *but through renegotiation we create further rules for how they ought to be used in the future.*

Changes in convictions can result from this combination of creation and discovery. Derek Black, born in 1989, was raised in a prominent white nationalist family; his father was the founder of the neo-Nazi website Stormfront. And Black was brought up to be a very active white supremacist himself—running (and being elected to) office in Florida, working on a radio show and at Stormfront with his father, and generally pushing a racist agenda. But during his college years, he changed his mind after forming a friendship with fellow student Matthew Stevenson, who invited Black to attend weekly Shabbat dinners.[9] Conversations with Black at these dinners were at first apolitical. But over time, trust developed, and they began to talk about racism.

During those conversations with Stevenson and others, Black began for the first time to really engage with the evidence undermining his views of white superiority. Moreover, he began to understand the consequences of those views—the kind of racial terror they led to. Before graduation, Black publicly renounced white supremacy. In a later op-ed in the *New York Times*, he described the transformation this way: "For me, the conversations that led me to change my views started because I couldn't understand why anyone would fear me. I thought I was only doing what was right and defending those I loved."[10] What happened is that he learned there were good reasons to fear racist ideology. These reasons made him abandon it—and to form a strong commitment to antiracism.

The reasons for Black's particular conversion are no doubt extremely complex.[11] But even the basic outlines of his case illustrate the importance of building trust, of reaching out, of dialogue—of not being arrogant. Black's change in conviction was the result of a reflective process of both tracking the evidence and testing his conviction for coherence against still deeper moral convictions. Among his foundational beliefs was the idea that he should not embrace harmful and frightening views. But he realized he *was* embracing such views—precisely because of the evidence brought before him. His new conviction still reflects the person he wants to be, but that's partly because he changed who he wants to be and partly because he realized he was confused about what kind of person he really was. He both discovered something—that his racist views were violating another conviction that he had—and created something, a new antiracist conviction.

Convictions reflect our self-identity, so they are difficult to change. Even talking about them can be delicate and feel like a betrayal, and explicit debate over our convictions with those who have opposing views can actually cause us to harden our views. But Black's case shows this isn't always so. When we approach our convictions with a Socratic attitude, when we are willing to improve and reshape our views by appeal to evidence and the experience of others, change is possible.

Intellectual Humility

These reflections suggest that there is a distinctive Socratic attitude toward how we should go about believing. It is, perhaps, the deepest legacy of philosophy, its one true and honest answer to the question of how to live. Montaigne and Hume strived, if imperfectly, to embody it. The American philosopher John Dewey would have called it open-mindedness; the educational establishment sometimes calls it critical thinking. But the best term for it might be "intellectual humility." It is not so much a trait as a kind of mental stance or orientation, one that we can hold more or less, and that can be reinforced or suppressed by our social conditions. It is not always valuable; it can be overblown or out of place. But it is a crucial attitude for inquiry and, I believe, for democracy itself. I'll define it as follows: *to be intellectually humble is to see your worldview as open to improvement from new evidence and the experience of others.*[12]

In order to see yourself as being able to improve from what others bring to the table, you can't think you know everything. You have to have absorbed the first Socratic lesson, and own your limitations. But being intellectually humble means more than admitting when you don't know. It means wanting to learn from the evidence and the experience of other people. That is why we treasure intellectual humility in our colleagues, our teammates, and our friends. And it is also what makes intellectual humility so important for democracy. As Dewey argued throughout his career, successful democratic politics requires constant work. We must work at mutual respect, and to do that we must work at listening and learning—to try to be open-minded, to be free "from prejudice, partisanship, and other such habits that close the mind and make it unwilling to consider new problems and entertain new ideas."[13] We need, in short, to be free from arrogance.

Socratic inquiry shows that intellectual humility involves caring about truth. For this reason, it is an attitude that is at the heart of science and philosophy. Perhaps more surprisingly, it is also an attitude that requires *confidence*. Socratic intellectual humility is not timidity in belief. And it is not the attitude of skepticism—at least, where that is understood to mean doubting that you know anything at all. In order to adopt Socratic humility, you can't be overly concerned about your ego. But that doesn't mean you lack an ego; you just don't put your ego before truth. To be open to learning from others, you need to be confident enough to realize what you know, and what you don't.

What all this tells us is that intellectual humility is not an opponent of conviction. To be open to improvement you must have a base to improve on. As Dewey remarked, this kind of attitude is "very different from empty-mindedness. While it is hospitality to new themes, facts, ideas, questions, it is not the kind of hospitality that would be indicated by hanging out a sign: 'Come right in; there is nobody at home.'"[14] In other words, listening to others, like a lot of things of value, is good, other things being equal. And things are not always equal.

Think about lying. Your mom no doubt taught you that honesty is the best policy. And it is. But policies have exceptions. When the Nazis are at the door looking for the Jews hidden in your attic, deceit is your only real option. The same holds for intellectual humility. You don't need to thoughtfully reconsider your views about racism when talking to the white supremacists on your doorstep. And one reason you don't has to do with the core meaning of intellectual humility. It means, in part, being open to the evidence supplied by the experience and testimony of others. But "evidence" here is key; just because someone comes up to you and says the Earth is flat doesn't mean you have to take that statement seriously. You can be intellectually humble without, to paraphrase a well-known expression, being so open-minded that your brain just falls out.

So, intellectual humility isn't timidity in belief. It isn't about servility either. The kind of humility I'm interested in isn't a matter of abasing yourself or seeing yourself as lower than others. It is not about giving up your convictions just because others, or the majority, think you must. As Socrates's own life makes plain, the pursuit of truth and the combating of arrogance often put you into conflict with those in power, simply because those in power are often the ones most resistant to challenges to the status quo and least able to recognize that they have confused ego with truth. That fact can often mean that who is being arrogant and who is being humble will be a matter of dispute.

Few events have stirred the pot of tribal arrogance in the United States more than the simple act of kneeling on a football field. During the 2016 season, Colin Kaepernick, a professional quarterback for the San Francisco 49ers, decided to protest what he considered to be disproportionate police violence against African Americans by kneeling during the singing of the national anthem at the start of the games in which he played. Kaepernick did not make speeches or give many interviews. He did not lecture. He just knelt.

The reaction to Kaepernick's protest is a textbook case of how the flames of arrogance and contempt are fed by the toxic combination of ideology and our digital platforms. But it also illustrates how one person's effort in humility can be portrayed as a display of arrogance. Kaepernick and many of the football players who joined him insisted that they didn't mean any disrespect to individual first responders or veterans. But that is not how their detractors and critics—including President Trump—saw their actions. To them, the kneelers were disrespecting the flag, as well as both service members and first responders. To his supporters, Kaepernick was humbly protesting racism and white arrogance. To his critics, he was arrogantly putting his politics before the respect owed to those in uniform.

Dissent has long been thought to have political value, at least in democracies. It is an expression of the freedom of thought and action that democracies value. But for Socrates, dissent also had value because it could be done in pursuit of truth. During his trial, Socrates posed to himself the question that was no doubt on the lips of many in Athens: why could he not just go away, keep silent, and live a quiet life? The answer, he suggested, was that to do so would have meant giving up on a central feature of a worthy life: inquiry. Ceasing his dissent would have meant giving up on pursuing what was true.

This seems an overstatement; as Aristotle implicitly suggested later, Socrates could have taken his inquiry, and his life, to different shores. Nonetheless, Socrates made an important point here: critical dissent is often a way to pursue politically important truth. It can, for example, act as a form of rational persuasion, as a way of laying out the evidence for thinking that a policy is flawed. That's why so many dissidents—from Thomas Paine to Marx—have used the pamphlet, essay, letter, book, or blog post to lay out their case against the policies of the powerful to those whom they hoped were still persuadable. The idea is that you can educate via the practices of dissent.

But protest and dissent can educate even when they do not persuade. The civil rights marchers in Birmingham and ACT UP protesters staging "die-ins" during the AIDS crisis weren't intending to change the minds of their most hardened opponents. They were seeking to raise the profile of an issue; to bring it to the attention of a public that wished to look away. Dissent can highlight the intellectual arrogance of the powerful. It can remind the privileged that they don't know everything. It can plant seeds of doubt. Acts of dissent can increase knowledge but also model a democratic way of pursuing it.

All of which makes Kaepernick's act of protest—and of those

who followed him—at once noble and saddening. Kaepernick himself was initially inclined to sit during the national anthem, but as was widely reported, a military veteran convinced him that it would be more respectful if he kneeled.[15] As that veteran, Mark Boyer, would later say in an interview, "We sorta came to a middle ground where he would take a knee alongside his teammates. . . . Soldiers take a knee in front of a fallen brother's grave, you know, to show respect."[16] It is therefore ironic that the act of kneeling—an action nearly universally seen as symbolic of humility and respect—is now viewed by many as a sign of the opposite qualities.

At least, that is the short-term reaction. Dissent, as any advocate of civil rights can tell you, has to play a long game. The general point I want to make here is that the Socratic attitude, the attitude of intellectual humility, is not antithetical to either conviction or critical political engagement. The opposite of intellectual humility is not conviction but the idea that we have no need of further inquiry, that our convictions are settled, and that no combination of future events could cause us to ever renegotiate their boundaries. The opposite is arrogance.

A Space of Reasons

Few philosophers are honored with their own stamp; John Dewey was, in 1968. A half century later, Dewey remains one of America's most influential thinkers, having contributed enormously to psychology, political theory, and most famously, education. But his star has faded in academic philosophy. As with Bertrand Russell, much of the discipline generally now just nods politely in Dewey's direction, every so often offering a tip of the cap with a citation here or there.

This is not too surprising. Dewey—again like Russell—was a giant of his time, and giants have a way of going in and out of fashion. But it is a shame, for Dewey thought long and hard about the themes of this book, and about truth and democracy in particular. In Dewey's pragmatist view, the value of truth is not something pure and golden, for truth itself cannot be strained away from the muddied waters of human interests. Truth always has a human face, and absolute certainty, Dewey thought, was an illusory goal whose pursuit in the political realm only encourages our worst instincts. "Truth," Dewey believed, "is important because of social interests."[17]

One of Dewey's driving ideas was that democracy is more than just a form of government; it is a way of life, "a conjoining of communicated experience."[18] Democracies, both Dewey and Hannah Arendt believed, aspire to be a kind of common space—a space where disagreements can be navigated without fear of violence or oppression. Democracies, we might say, are spaces of reasons.[19]

I have urged in these pages that this conception of democracy is essentially grounded on the even more basic ideal of respect for persons.[20] Again, the point is that in democratic politics one regards one's fellow citizens as autonomous and worthy of equal

KNOW-IT-ALL SOCIETY

respect. That means treating them as capable of making up their own minds. And we treat our fellow citizens with respect when we see them as capable of making these judgments on the basis of reasons—*even when, in fact, we know that nonrational forces often rule the day.* That's why we feel squeamish about manipulative political advertising, even when it is on our "side." Getting people to agree with us is not all that matters. How we reach agreement also matters. As we saw in Chapter 5, as tempting as it might be to release a drug into the water that would get everyone thinking as you do about politics, it would be wrong to do so because the act would violate basic respect, basic human dignity.

To see democracy as a space of reasons is to regard the ideals of democratic politics as requiring a commitment to pursuit of the truth. But not in just any way—for example, in complete disregard for human welfare (as Nazi scientists did, for example, in experimenting on Jewish prisoners). The particularly democratic value attached to the pursuit of truth lies in *the manner in which democracies promote and protect these pursuits* by ensuring rights of free assembly, speech, a free press, and the norms of academic freedom.[21] "The essential need, in other words, is the improvement of the methods and conditions of debate, discussion and persuasion," Dewey noted. "That is *the* problem of the public."[22]

In this, I believe Dewey is exactly right. The space of reasons that democracies need is a common public discourse. That's why Dewey believed that democracies should encourage institutions that engage in inquiry in a way that improves the "conditions" of discourse. It's what makes artistic, scientific, historical, legal,

and journalistic institutions so essential. They construct the public space of reasons by providing reasons; they pursue truth not
through fiat but by prizing evidence and inquiry. In encouraging
these institutions, democracies hope to increase the public stock
of knowledge. But the point I take from Dewey is that the true
democratic value of these institutions lies in the fact that they
embody the open, public *pursuit* of that knowledge. It is their
pursuit of truth via open, transparent, and deliberative inquiry
that makes them part of the practice of democracy.

It can be easy to misunderstand this point. Plato thought that
the typical citizen in a democracy is an unreliable pursuer of truth:

Sometimes he drinks heavily while listening to the flute; at
other times, he drinks only water and is on a diet; sometimes he goes in for physical training; at other times, he's
idle and neglects everything.[23]

Plato notoriously thought this meant that governance should
be handed over to philosopher-kings. They would be able to
acquire political knowledge, and then disseminate it, as needed,
to the other citizens. The net effect, he thought, would be a better-
informed citizenry. Current autocratic governments make similar arguments in defense of restrictions on speech and online
searches. By weeding out so-called false influences, they say, these
restrictions make it easier for citizens to access the truth.

This argument misses its mark on two fronts. First, the virtues
of the philosopher-king have a way of becoming the vices of the

tyrant. Intellectual arrogance comes for us all, and any mechanism that makes knowledge the province of a few will inevitably grind to a halt because of that fact. Second, Dewey's point isn't about the individual alone. One can agree with Plato that we are all generally terrible inquirers. We lurch off the road to truth at the least distraction. But that fact only makes Dewey's point. The space of reasons, a space of discourse that allows for the pursuit of truth, aims to be built in a way that corrects for the crooked timber of its materials—that is, to be constructed out of practices that aim to correct for the biases of their individual participants. To put it plainly, just as Socrates advises that we individual citizens pursue truth with an attitude of intellectual humility, so should democracies bolster those institutions—science, education, the media—that encourage the pursuit of truth in similar ways.

But what ways are those? The question is complex, but I think it's clear that we should urge those institutions that engage in inquiry to promote the use of what I'll call "reflective practices." Reflective practices get us to focus on how we think and, in particular, how we believe.

Reflective practices are not as exotic as they sound. In his book *The Checklist Manifesto*, Atul Gawande details the struggles in getting doctors to use checklists before surgery.[24] The checklists were intended to prevent errors, including, for example, removing the wrong limb. Somewhat surprisingly, surgeons had resisted this practice for years. Following a checklist, many doctors had argued, was unnecessary; they were highly trained experts and they didn't want to be lulled into a false sense of security that a completed checklist might provide. None of these arguments turned out to be very persuasive. Data subsequently collected in a series of studies showed that checklists saved lives. Not surprisingly either, other professionals—airline pilots, for example—had used checklists for decades.

The case illustrates how intellectual arrogance can tempt the best of us, and how we can combat it. Using a checklist helps us combat arrogance because a checklist is a reflective practice. A checklist is designed not to help you know new information; it helps you check on whether you know what you think you do. Are you amputating the right leg or the left? Is there sufficient fuel for the trip? These are important questions for surgeons and pilots, and if they are well trained and competent, of course, they don't need a checklist to know the answers. But that's not the point. The point of the checklist is not to *answer* those questions but to help people check on their answers. And in so doing, it does one other really important thing: a checklist reminds us of our own fallibility—and therefore combats arrogance by training us to remember that we don't always know what we think we do.

There is another aspect of these two examples that makes them relevant for our purposes. Pilots and surgeons are similar in at least three important respects: their jobs take immense concentration, they require quick decision-making in often stressful situations, and the cost of a mistake can be extraordinarily high. It is not surprising, therefore, that both professions attract very similar sorts of personalities: people who are bright, cool under fire, and not prone to second-guessing themselves. These are qualities you want in people who have those sorts of jobs. You want them to be highly trained and to have a high degree of self-trust—to not be hesitant.

Yet it is not difficult to imagine that these same qualities can also encourage intellectual arrogance. If you are told you are good at making quick, tough decisions and then acting on them, you may come to confuse the basis of your self-trust. You might start thinking you are right just because you are, well, you. (That doesn't mean that pilots or surgeons are always arrogant, of course.) The checklist can work against that tendency, just as the more humdrum checklists that the rest of us use do. Checklists serve as a constant reminder of our fallibility.

Another salient part of Gawande's story of the checklist is that checklists, once institutionalized, become part of the social background of that institution. The social background of an institution is the set of norms and practices that its participants take for granted, that they assume as part of its normal functioning. When professionally institutionalized, following a checklist is a reflective practice that becomes part of the social background for people working in those professions. That's the reason it can encourage humility—or one aspect of intellectual humility. It works away in the background even when the *individuals* involved are intellectually arrogant and thus are less-than-ideal pursuers of truth.

Other reflective practices also do this—practices that are scalable and can be enshrined in institutions. For example, training to raise awareness of sexual harassment and implicit bias is a reflective practice. If done well, training like this gets us to focus on not

only our actions but also our habits of mind, our assumptions—
our mind-set. It reminds us of our fallibility, but it also encourages us to take seriously the experiences of other people. Another
example is fact-checking practices in journalism. The news media
not only gets us information. It also serves as a key reflective function society-wide: it is the "watchdog" that checks on both itself
and the pronouncements of those in power, and it does that in part
through fact-checking. As such, the news media, too, can combat
arrogance by reminding us of the fallibility of the powerful. And
as I've already argued, peaceful protest and critical dissent can
also act in the same way. All of these practices can make us more
aware of how we approach the world, and of the assumptions that
we bring with us.

Ultimately, the question of *which* reflective practices we
should make part of the social background is an empirical one.
The philosophical point is that reflective practices *can and are used
to encourage intellectual humility at the level of institutions*. And
that is a hopeful idea.

To resolve disputes and achieve consensus, democracies need
a common currency of reasons and evidence to trade in. The edi-
fices of inquiry just discussed—a free press, scientific, artistic, and
educational institutions, and so on—collectively form the mint
for this currency. They aim to provide us with evidence and the
means to appreciate it that enable us to trade in reasons. And these
institutions are made better, are improved in their basic function,
when they put reflective practices into their social background.

Without such institutions and practices, democracy suffers,

and that is why we should be so concerned about the attacks mounted on them by tyrants the world over. By harming the institutions that are our best shield against tribal arrogance, those attacks contribute to its spread. We form our opinions within a community; when things are going right, we trust each other as sources of expertise, and we trust in the institutions—the media, science—meant to assist in that process. But once we start becoming tribally arrogant know-it-alls, trust breaks down because the tribally arrogant dismiss evidence as fake news and label any institution that supports it an enemy of the people.

And sadly, the reverse also holds. To the extent that experts are themselves arrogant *or perceived to be so*, they can lose the trust of the very people who need them. That's why it can be a mistake for scientists to ignore climate-change skeptics, to refuse to debate them or not bother to direct critical fire at their arguments. I say this while fully realizing that giving credence to a criticism, legitimate or otherwise, can increase its visibility and possibly lead to more people taking it seriously. But try to suppress a criticism, and public discourse finds a way of bringing it back up. This is how the ideologies of arrogance corrupt reasonable discourse: they make it so that both responding to criticism and not responding to it end up undermining democratic attitudes and ideals.

The overall argument I've pulled from Socrates and Dewey is this: the Socratic lesson is that our best hope for believing with integrity is to pursue truth with the attitude of intellectual humility. That attitude consists in both owning one's limitations and being willing to learn from the experience of others. But it is also what is required by the ideal of democracy as a space of reasons. That ideal takes the pursuit of truth as an essential democratic good, embodied in those social practices and institutions that promote intellectually humble inquiry. That's why these same institutions—the press, science education, peaceful dissent—are the best defense against tribal arrogance. It is also why they are the most threatened by it.

To some, this will sound like a precarious argument. Truth, one might think, is too airy a notion, too intangible, on which to even partly found democracy. It is to this skepticism—skepticism about truth itself—that I now turn.

Truth and Democracy

"Truth isn't truth," a spokesperson for the president remarked not long ago, capturing in one bizarre moment the essence of not only the administration's hostile relationship with reality, but the "post-truth" attitude eating away at the foundations of our democracy. Strictly speaking, of course, there is no such thing as being "post-truth." Truth *is* truth, no matter what politicians might say. But the post-truth *attitude*, on the other hand, is real.

One reason for this attitude is the simple fact that we live in a digital world that makes it both easier and harder to figure out what is true. That very fact, if we aren't careful, can lead us into thinking that objectivity is a dead value. We get so used to contradictory information, rival sources, that we can talk ourselves into thinking truth is irrelevant.

We've already encountered relativism about truth—an old idea that goes back at least as far as the ancient Greek rhetorician Protagoras, who held that objective truth was an illusion because "man is the measure of all things." But the kind of cynicism about truth now at work in our political culture is importantly different from Protagoras's theory. The relativist can still think truth is important; it is just relative. This stance is different from dismissing the importance of truth altogether.

To some, skepticism about truth sounds like a sophisticated bit of political realism. Talk of truth is for the loser; alternative facts are for winners. To others, who confuse truth with entrenched belief, such skepticism may seem liberating, freeing us from what others take for granted. Neither attitude is particularly compelling. Truth does not pick winners and losers, and just because most people believe something does not guarantee that it is true any more than it guarantees that it is wise or just. And the inference from "we cannot agree, therefore truth is irrelevant" is just fallacious. In its simplest form, it confuses the difficulty of being certain with the impossibility of truth. It is always difficult to know for certain what is true. Maybe you really live in the Matrix. Maybe you have a brain chip implant feeding you all the wrong information. But in practice, we do all agree on some facts: that bullets kill people, that you can't flap your arms and fly.

Maybe, however, our agreement on some facts shows that it is agreement, after all, that we are after. One of the twentieth

century's most distinguished and brilliant philosophers, Richard
Rorty, would sometimes put things that way:

> The grounding premise of my argument is that you cannot
> aim at something, cannot work to get it, unless you can rec-
> ognize it once you have got it. . . . We shall never know for
> sure whether a given belief is true, but we can be sure that
> nobody is presently able to summon up any residual objec-
> tions to it, that everybody agrees that it ought to be held.[25]

In sum, truth cannot be a target of inquiry, because we can
never know whether we've hit it. And a target we can't know
we've hit is no target at all. Yet we can know whether "every-
body agrees" with a belief. Therefore, agreement or consensus,
not truth, is the proper aim of inquiry. It is what we really aim
at in politics and in life.

I am more than happy to agree that agreement is important.
This book, after all, has been driven by the worry that our penchant for intellectual arrogance is only deepening political disagreement. But that doesn't mean agreement is the only thing that
matters. What we agree about on Monday we may not agree about
on Tuesday. And the fact that we do agree on some proposition is
no guarantee that it is true. Agreement is just a sign that we may
be closer to the truth—an indication, not a sure bet.

There is an old philosophical problem about happiness—
arguably going back to the Greeks: that you can't pursue happiness directly because when you do, you invariably make yourself

less happy. If you explicitly do things—make friends, engage in a career, and so on—only as a means to your own happiness, you are bound to find that happiness slipping away. Ask yourself whether you are happy, John Stuart Mill once remarked in his autobiography, putting a fine point on the matter, and you'll discover you are not. The solution, it is often thought, is to pursue it indirectly, to treat happiness as a by-product of activities—friendship, for example—that are good in themselves. Happiness emerges, but only indirectly from the pursuit of other things.

Truth, in certain ways, is like happiness. You can't pursue it directly. Ask yourself whether your beliefs are really true and you may find, as Descartes and Montaigne both did, that it is extremely hard to believe anything at all. But that doesn't mean we should give up on truth any more than we should give up on happiness. It just means we must pursue it indirectly.

To take another example, think of the relationship between economic growth and investment. Countries want their wealth to grow. But to make that happen, they must invest in sound policies. The immediate goal is to find out which policies are wise or sound. That doesn't mean that the ultimate goal is not economic growth; it just means you can't get to one without the other—even though, sadly, one can follow wise policies and still end up underwater.

Likewise, truth is the ultimate end of inquiry, but we don't pursue it directly. We pursue it instead indirectly, by pursuing evidence that supplies us with reasons for belief. Indirectly or not, however, it is truth that supplies the point of the pursuit, and truth that distinguishes it from merely pursuing whatever rallies others to our cause or flatters our opinions. Truth is also what distinguishes the pursuit of evidence from the practice of answering objections—that is, from the practice of simply saying whatever silences your opponent, or gets them to nod in agreement. Reasons are important in and of themselves. But reasons for a belief are *reasons* precisely because they are not mere means to their own end; they are means to the further end of truth. Thus, like agreement, reason giving is distinct from truth precisely as a means is distinct from its end.

Still, truth can seem a mysterious and paradoxical concept— or just too "airy" to have any real use. Pontius Pilate's rhetorical query "What is truth?" echoes the implicit views of many people that it is not really a question we can answer. If not, then perhaps the skeptic is on to something after all. This second kind of skepticism about truth is often encouraged by a kind of all-or-nothing approach to understanding what truth is: it either has one explicable nature or none at all.

Many philosophers throughout history have assumed, with Gottfried Leibniz, that we should be "content with looking for truth in the correspondence between the propositions which are in the mind and the things which they are about."[26] Truth is a relationship between mind and world, and that relationship is a kind of correspondence or matching. If we think of the world as consisting of facts, such as the fact that there is a cat on my mat, or that grass is green, and so on, then in order to be true, our thoughts must correspond to some independent objective fact. Thus, it is true that there is a cat on the mat when there is, in fact, a real cat on a real mat.

The "correspondence theory" of truth, as it has come to be called, is a very reasonable view when dealing with propositions about cats, mats, grass, and the other middle-sized physical objects in our environment. The problem is that, as philosophers from Nietzsche onward are fond of pointing out, it is less easy to see which physical facts mathematical, economic, or moral beliefs correspond to. Yet it is still *true* that there is no such thing as a free lunch, or that 2 and 2 make 4, or that sexual harassment is morally wrong. Hence, some philosophers have thought that the correspondence theory of truth, being inapplicable to such beliefs, must be wrong. But if you think that the correspondence theory is the only way to understand truth, then you may be apt to think that the whole concept is confused.

That, in my view, is throwing the baby out with the bathwater. One doesn't have to think that there is one and only one way for our various kinds of beliefs to be true. No rule says that truth and knowledge in morality must be as they are in physics.[27] But putting the metaphysics aside, the *concept* of truth—the basic idea—is not all that difficult to understand.

To grasp the concept of objective truth, you really only need to see two points. First, believing doesn't make it so. We can't just make up facts because that is what we want the world to be like. Otherwise, life would be a lot easier than it is. Second, to paraphrase Hamlet's warning to Horatio, there are more things under heaven and earth than are dreamt of in your PowerPoint presentation. There will always be facts we don't know about. Consider, to take a trivial example, the proposition that the number of stars in the universe right now is odd. That is a fact or it isn't, since the number will be either even or odd. If it is a fact, we'll never know, because the vast distances in the universe and the laws of physics concerning the speed of light mean that even if we ran around at the speed of light and counted all the stars we could see, many would have turned to dust millions of years earlier by the time we were done counting. And of course there are many facts like this, about the distant past, about far parts of the universe, about numbers that are extraordinarily complex. No one can know it all.

Put those ideas together and you get, "If something is true, it doesn't mean you'll believe it; and if you believe something, that doesn't mean it is true." Understand those two points and you understand what it means to talk about the objectivity of truth.

This is also the essence of intellectual humility. You don't know it all, because the truth is independent of your ego. It is also why both ideas are so important and why they are so hard to achieve. To strive after truth and humility means that we must always be ready to consider new evidence and new experiences, and that we cannot rest content in our convictions. Part of being intellectually humble is treating truth, not just agreement, as a goal of inquiry. And part of the value of humility lies in the antecedent value of truth.

Yet this fact also reminds us of the political value of both concepts. In Orwell's *1984*, the protagonist, Winston Smith, is tortured by the thought policeman O'Brien until he agrees that 2 plus 2 equals 5. The point, O'Brien explains, is to make Smith see that there is no truth other than what the party says is true. What O'Brien knows is that once that premise is accepted, dissent, even critical thought, becomes literally impossible. You can't speak truth to power if power speaks truth by definition.

This very reason is why it is crucial to slow down the spread of tribal arrogance—especially among those of us convinced we wear the armor of righteousness. It is also why we should not give up on truth and humility, and why neither information pollution nor polarization should make us abandon them. When we own what we don't know and remain open to what others do, we exemplify a basic respect for our fellow citizens that is demanded by democracy. We may never completely realize the ideal of respect—the ideal of living in a society that treats people equally, that achieves social justice, that values truth and reasons, and that rejects arrogance and dogmatism. But these are goals worth striving for, and it would be perverse to give up on them just when they are under threat. It is precisely then that democratic ideals matter most.

Acknowledgments

FEW things bring home the realization that you don't know very much than the act of writing a book. The writing of this book was no exception. I benefited from the comments, advice, and support of a great number of people and institutions.

Work on the book was supported by a generous grant from the John Templeton Foundation, and by the University of Connecticut and the whole team at Humility & Conviction in Public Life, a multidisciplinary research and engagement project at UConn.

Many of these ideas were first voiced as talks at the College de France, the Norwegian Academy of Sciences and Letters, the Free University of Amsterdam, Oxford University, the University of Copenhagen, the Institute of Philosophy in London, the Episteme Conference, Mount Aloysius College, Franklin & Marshall College, Cardiff University, Georgetown University, Harvard University, and the University of Pennsylvania. I benefited greatly from comments given by each of these audiences. Portions of Chapter 1 are based on work that appeared as "Arrogance, Truth and Public Discourse" in *Episteme* in 2018. The first section of Chapter 2 leans on research done for "Can We Be Reasonable?" coauthored with Teresa Allen; work with Hanna Gunn informed portions of the same chapter.

Over the last few years I've learned a considerable amount from Jason Baehr, Donald Baxter, Paul Bloom, Paul Bloomfield, Alexis Boylan, Pascal Engel, Manuela Fabiani, Anke Finger, Brandon Fitelson, Thomas Foley, Karen Frost-Arnold, Sandy Goldberg, Matthew Guariglia, Hanna Gunn, Casey Rebecca Johnson, Brendan Kane, Jason Kawall, Frank Keil, Nathan Kellen, Junyeol Kim, Jennifer Lackey, Tracy Llanara, Dana Miranda, Duncan Pritchard, Nathan Sheff, Steve Sloman, and Lynne Tirell. I'd also like to acknowledge the work of Quassim Cassam, whose book on parallel themes alas came out too late to discuss in these pages.

Teresa Allen, James Beebe, Jason Kawall, and Toby Napoletano provided feedback on very early drafts of several chapters; Terry Berthelot, Paul Bloomfield, and Micki McElya provided much-needed help with later versions. Heather Battaly and Alessandra Tanesini taught me much about virtues and attitudes (although they may not think I learned enough). Of particular help were my writing mentors Patty Lynch and Kent Stephens; my agent, Peter Matson; my terrific copy editor, Stephanie Hiebert; and my editor, Robert Weil, who saved me from myself.

My last thanks as always are to Terry and Kathleen, who have taught me that life and learning should be acts not only of determination but of joy.

Notes

Preamble: No Ordinary Question

1. Plato 1992, 352d.
2. See, in particular, Pew Research Center 2016 and Pew Research Center 2017.
3. Camus 1956, 239–40.
4. Arendt 2006, 252.
5. Throughout the book, I somewhat reluctantly use the word "tribe" to denote groups whose members share a common set of political convictions in the sense I define below—that is, a shared self-identity. The word is not perfect—it carries the baggage of colonialism—but it does convey that such groups—such as white nationalists, or liberal philosophy professors—are not "mere" groups but people connected by strands of identity.
6. Russell 1935, 11.

Chapter 1: Montaigne's Warning

1. Montaigne 2003, 557, 543.
2. A recent and comprehensive biography by Philippe Desan stresses these points, and the relationship between Montaigne's philosophy and his political life. See Desan 2017.

3. Montaigne 2003, 495.
4. Montaigne 2003, 693.
5. Montaigne 2003, 557.
6. See Dunning 2011.
7. See Rozenblit and Keil 2002. Keil's work on the psychology of knowledge in particular has been groundbreaking.
8. A related and important series of results comes from Steve Sloman and his colleague Phil Fernbach (Sloman and Fernbach 2017). Their results indicate that when there is knowledge out in the community on a given topic—or even if we just think there is—we often blur the line between what's inside our heads and what's not. We overestimate how much we *individually* know because we conflate our individual knowledge with what we believe is common knowledge. We fall into thinking that all that common knowledge is common in our head too. *Somebody* knows how zippers work, so we must too. See also Keil et al. 2008.
9. Montaigne 2003, 674.
10. Many cognitive scientists working today agree. And while these systems are often now called (following economist Daniel Kahneman) "system 1" and "system 2," the older terms "intuition" and "reflection" are more descriptive. Kornblith (2012) makes the case that our trust in our individual reflection is often overrated. This is surely correct, but as I argue later, reflective social practices are useful nonetheless.
11. See Kahneman 2011.
12. This tendency to take shortcuts in judgments starts at a very young age: infants compare and contrast new objects (for example, a novel ball) with objects they have experience with (for example, familiar balls), and make assumptions about the new objects on this basis. See Baldwin et al. 1993. For a relevant discussion, see Leslie 2017.
13. Hume 1999, 101.
14. See Banaji 2002, esp. 151–52.
15. For a discussion of all three of these points, see Gendler 2011, 39–40.
16. See Gendler 2011, 38–41.
17. The use of "we" here is deliberate. Regrettably, the stereotypes that influence and infect the way we categorize people are numerous; it is not difficult to think up other similar examples and the data suggests we are all susceptible, whether or not we belong to the group we are categorizing.
18. In one study, subjects, independently of race, identified guns faster, and also

misidentified tools as guns more often, when primed by nonwhite faces than they did when primed with white faces. The widely accepted explanation for this result is that the subjects were more likely to associate blackness with danger than they were to associate whiteness with danger. See Payne 2001, 187. For more on attitudes and self-presentational strategies, see Dunton and Fazio 1997; Fazio et al. 1995; and Greenwald et al. 1998.

19. The research on this phenomenon is abundant; see G. L. Cohen 2003, Dana and Loewenstein 2003, Dovidio and Gaertner 1991 and 2004, Epley and Dunning 2000, Heath 1999, Miller and Ratner 1998, Pronin et al. 2007, Robinson et al. 1995, Uhlmann and Cohen 2007, and Vivian and Berkowitz 1992.

20. Hume (1888) 1978, 597.

21. Ricks 2006, 99.

22. This is a point first made in Tanesini 2016a. The present account owes clear debts to Tanesini's groundbreaking work. Compare also Gordon 2016 (p. 6): "The rule of opinion over truth and evidence is a form of revolt of the soul against reality."

23. As the preceding discussion in the text has underscored, intellectual arrogance here is not being understood as a trait, although nothing precludes there being traits that cause people to be epistemically arrogant. A trait is a stable dispositional quality of a person—dispositional in the sense that someone can have the trait even when failing to overtly exhibit it, and stable in that one does not typically have a trait on Monday but lack it on Tuesday. A personality trait is part of one's psychological architecture, so to speak. Attitudes can also be dispositional. One can have the attitude of contempt toward something even if that thing does not always rise to conscious attention. The contempt can be implicit. But unlike traits, attitudes need not be stable across time.

24. Montaigne 2003, 484.

Chapter 2: The Outrage Factory

1. For more on Google-knowing, see Gunn and Lynch 2019, and Lynch 2016.

2. See Fisher et al. 2015.

3. Fisher et al. 2015, 675.

4. See Goldman 2016.

5. See Stanley 2015.

6. As I write this, Facebook has uncovered a coordinated network of fake accounts aimed at election interference. The numbers tell the story of social

media's power to contribute to pollution: while only thirty pages and accounts were flagged for such deception, just under 300,000 people were following them. See Fandos and Roose 2018.

7. I take this point to be a demonstration of Sandy Goldberg's important argument that the reliability of this inference depends on the epistemic health of the relevant social practices and institutions. See S. Goldberg 2010, 154ff.

8. For an extremely insightful discussion of close-mindedness, see Battaly 2018b.

9. Compare Kidd 2018.

10. See Farhi 2016.

11. Compare Rini (2017), who argues that sharing content online is a form of what she calls "bent testimony." In the analysis that I provide in the text, I agree that our acts of sharing news stories can constitute acts of testimony, but I argue that testimony is not the *primary function* of those acts, an idea influenced by the seminal work of Ruth Millikan.

12. Gabielkov et al. 2016.

13. And it may go even further than that, as I once heard a senior Facebook representative (off the record) acknowledge that the company's own data showed that the problem was actually much greater: as much as 90 percent of the stories shared on that platform may not be clicked through by those sharing them.

14. See C. Dewey 2016.

15. Brady et al. 2017.

16. Crockett 2018. See also Crockett 2017.

17. As earlier, I use "assertion" here as a shorthand for "assertion of something factual or descriptive"; and "endorsement" as an act (possibly of assertion, depending on one's underlying semantic theory) of normative recommendation, as in, "One ought to rely on this source." My notion of a "primary function" is derived from Millikan's (2017) notion of a stabilizing function.

18. I've been particularly influenced by Dorit Bar-On's thoughts on expressivism (Bar-On and Chrisman 2009). See Blackburn 1998, Chrisman 2008, Ridge 2014, and Schroeder 2008 for additional important presentations of expressivism. The version I endorse bears affinities to so-called double-aspect accounts, according to which communicative acts can have both descriptive and expressive aspects to their content.

19. As the philosopher Karen Frost-Arnold says in a forthcoming manuscript (Frost-Arnold 2018), this can, in turn, undermine "the social practices of objectivity." I will return to this point myself in the coming chapters.

Chapter 3: Where the Spade Turns

1. Wittgenstein 1969, sec. 94.
2. Wittgenstein 1969, sec. 204.
3. Emerson 2000, 264. @realDonaldTrump tweeted the quote on April 10, 2014.
4. The phrase "convictions are the wellsprings of doctrine" is borrowed from Walzer 2006, 114.
5. For related research on the role that conviction plays in political motivation, see Skitka et al. 2005.
6. Despite the importance of conviction for our moral and political lives, there has been surprisingly little direct attention on the topic in the history of philosophy—perhaps because philosophers are often shy around commitment and their semiprofessional role of public skeptics. Independent of some of the examples mentioned in the text, relatively recent work includes Skitka et al. 2005, Pianalto 2011, and some penetrating remarks in Williams 1985.
7. This conception of caring comes from Frankfurt 1988.
8. See Williams 1985, 169.
9. The fact that convictions require this kind of commitment—even when characterized subjunctively, as in the text—means that we aren't necessarily committed to every proposition logically entailed by our convictions.
10. I owe this point, and much else on this subject, to James Beebe.
11. Flanagan 1996, 67. See also Dennett 2014.
12. MacIntyre 2013, 219.
13. I do not mean, in presenting these cultural narratives in binary terms, to suggest that they capture the full range of intersecting identities that we humans actually inhabit. But I do intend to capture the stifling way in which dominant cultural narratives tend to reinforce those binaries.
14. As the philosopher Bernard Williams once drolly noted, a man might deeply value his membership in MENSA without that constituting his identity; and if it did, we would think him in a bad way. See Williams 1985, 169–70.
15. Hochschild 2018, 135.
16. Wittgenstein 1969, sec. 613.
17. Skitka et al. 2005.
18. Nietzsche 2005, 55.
19. See Dunlap and McCright 2008, and McCright and Dunlap 2011. See also the discussion in Jost 2015.
20. Lynch 2012b.

21. See Kahan 2013, and Kahan et al. 2007 and 2012.
22. Greene 2014, 94.
23. See Kahan 2013, and Kahan et al. 2012.
24. See Menand 2001–2.

Chapter 4: Ideologies of Arrogance and the American Right

1. Arendt 1966, 304.
2. Arendt 1966, 348.
3. See Snyder 2015.
4. Arendt 1966, 360. Indeed, the SS even tried to expunge the word "nation" from the Nazis' propaganda.
5. Arendt 1966, 324.
6. Arendt 1966, 324.
7. Arendt 1966, 348.
8. Arendt 1966, 349.
9. Arendt 1966, 350.
10. Strang 2017, xiv.
11. Strang 2017, xiv.
12. Strang 2017, xiv.
13. Strang 2017, 174.
14. Strang 2017, 175.
15. Hochschild 2018, 228.
16. Strang 2017, 174.
17. Frank 2016.
18. Clinton's use of the term "deplorables" has interestingly been stripped of its context by most reporting. Made at an LGBT fundraiser in New York, the remark was embedded in a longer argument for the claim that many Trump supporters had legitimate economic complaints. Ironically, seen in the context of the full transcript (Reilly 2016), the remark can be seen as an apparent attempt to acknowledge what I'm calling both the cultural and the economic explanation.
19. See Mutz 2018.
20. Some conservatives are no doubt fooling themselves on this point, just as many liberals are fooling themselves about their own racism. You never learn much about racial attitudes in America by simply asking people, "Are you racist?" Ascriptions of racism don't work that way.
21. Mutz 2018, 3.
22. Mutz 2018, 7.

23. Arendt 1966, 227.

24. See Sharockman 2017.

25. For the former quote, see Reeve 2017; for the latter, see Beavers 2017.

26. See Medina 2012. The foundational text for work on ignorance is Mills 1997. See also Polhaus 2012, and Gordon 1995 and 2000.

27. Stanley 2018, 21–22.

28. Kate Manne stresses the moral delusion at the heart of misogyny and sexism. See Manne 2018, 157–58.

29. Gordon 2000.

30. The comparison with bad faith is due to the seminal account of philosopher Lewis Gordon, who applied the concept to racism: "An important aspect of a person in bad faith is his uncritical attitude toward evidence he favors and his critical attitude toward evidence that displeases him . . . to hear that blacks and Indians are savages is one thing; to accept that as a given truth is another. To continue accepting that they are supposed to be incapable of achieving feats that one regards as high human achievements in light of the countless alternative interpretations available . . . makes the acceptance a downright form of denial" (Gordon 2000, 4). For a full development of this view, see Gordon 1995.

31. Arendt 1966, 382.

32. Such a commitment may, of course, also reflect what an epistemically arrogant person believes to be true. That is, she might be committed to the unimprov-ability of her epistemic state (or some aspect of it) because she really believes it is unimprovable. But she might not too. In that case, the unwillingness and the accompanying commitment may be due to the arrogant person's realizing—if only implicitly—that she is vulnerable to criticism. In such a case, she does not *believe* her view is unimpeachable but still takes the attitude of the know-it-all because of self-defensiveness or insecurity.

33. Those in the grip of this delusion could, at an even farther extreme, also act on the idea that if p, then they believe p. If so (again assuming classical negation), then, put together with the principle cited in the text ("if he believes p, then p"), this would amount to the truly bizarre view that they believe p if, and only if, p.

34. See Battaly 2018a and 2018b.

Chapter 5: Liberalism and the Philosophy of Identity Politics

1. See Meckler 2018.

2. J. Goldberg 2018, 211.

3. Lilla 2017, 10.

NOTES

4. The statement can be found, among other places, on the collective's website: Combahee River Collective, "Combahee River Collective Statement," accessed January 19, 2019, https://combaheerivercollective.weebly.com/the -combahee-river-collective-statement.html.

5. Lilla 2017, 85.

6. J. Goldberg 2018, 217.

7. Schmitt 2008, 29.

8. "Combahee River Collective Statement." Mychal Denzal Smith makes this same point in Smith 2017.

9. The argument here is clearly indebted to that made by Taylor (1994); see especially pages 30–35. In particular, my own account of the formation of self-identities agrees with Taylor's conception of human beings as essentially dialogical in nature. But where I read Taylor as somewhat ambivalent about the relationship between respect and recognition, I argue in the text for a close interconnection.

10. Not all critics of identity politics do conflate the two. Indeed, Lukianoff and Haidt (2018) also distinguish between what they call "common-humanity" versus "common-enemy" approaches to identity politics.

11. Fraser 2000.

12. See, for example, Alcoff 2007.

13. See, for example, Harding 1991 and 1993. Still one of the best overviews of this subject is Alessandra Tanesini's brilliant *Introduction to Feminist Epistemologies* (1999).

14. See Paul 2014.

15. See Haslanger 2014.

16. Rorty 1979.

17. Harding 1993, 61.

18. "Liberal Arrogance," Conservapedia, accessed January 19, 2019, https://www .conservapedia.com/Liberal_arrogance.

19. Grim 2016.

20. Rensin 2016.

21. Oakeshott 1991, 6.

22. Thus I wish I had entitled an earlier book *In Praise of Reasons*.

23. Fingerhut 2017.

24. See, for example, Jaschik 2016 and 2017.

25. As the director of a research institute, I know that this is incorrect. Professors in the humanities and social sciences are still working on the same sorts of

periods, topics, and issues that their graduate advisers worked on. Early modern history is still big, as is metaphysics; so, humanities fields, while filled with liberals, are not "dominated" by those working on gender or racial issues.

26. See Pew Research Center 2009.

27. P. Cohen 2008.

28. The solution, I think, is not going to be as simple as calling for more "viewpoint diversity" on faculties (a term I don't really understand) or as drastic as calling for affirmative action policies for the hiring of conservative academics. These latter proposals, while setting off alarms around liberal academy, are particularly unserious, since (1) it is not clear they would be constitutional; (2) they are deeply impractical, since, ironically, it would fall on largely liberal professors to judge whether a colleague is "conservative" or not; and (3) conservatives largely oppose them anyway.

29. The points in this paragraph draw from work by Robin Dillon (2003, 2015) and Stephen Darwall (2006, 2013).

30. This is a point driven home in Talisse, forthcoming. For his views on democracy and disagreement, see Talisse 2009.

31. Compare the philosopher Macalester Bell's treatment of "apt contempt" in Bell 2013. I don't deny that some degree of contempt may be morally apt in certain cases; my point is that contempt always lacks democratic political value.

Chapter 6: Truth and Humility as Democratic Values

1. Plato 1928b, 486.

2. Plato 1928a, 64.

3. Te-Tao Ching, sec. 71; see, for example, Hendricks 2010.

4. This observation is the central argument of Whitcomb et al. 2015.

5. In these pursuits, a dialogue can establish a kind of trust that can make subsequent discussion more effective. Numerous nonprofits teach such techniques across the nation to schools, community groups, and businesses, helping them to encourage constructive communication, often over divisive issues. The particulars of their models vary, but many involve training people to actively listen and empathize across differences. For a list of resources assembled by expert Brendan Kane, see: Humility and Conviction in Public Life: https://humilityandconviction.uconn.edu. In addition, see, for example, these organizations, all accessed January 19, 2019: Essential Partners, https://whatisessential.org/workshop/power-dialogue-constructive-conversations-divisive-issues; the

Sustained Dialogue Institute, https://sustaineddialogue.org; and the National Institute for Civil Discourse https://nicd.arizona.edu.

6. On this point I am influenced by Davidson 2005.

7. Moreover, the concept itself doesn't dictate a single answer—although it will rule out many as incorrect. See Lynch 1998.

8. For further developments of Wittgenstein's views as they apply to political theory, see Pitkin 1972.

9. Saslow 2016.

10. Black 2016.

11. I owe Tracy Llanera for pointing out some of those complexities.

12. "Intellectual humility" is a technical term whose meaning and reference is still under negotiation within both philosophy and psychology. Like many other technical terms, it has been introduced in the hope of more perfectly picking out assorted phenomena that are only imperfectly picked out by ordinary language. Rather than attempting to adjudicate these discussions, I have tried to indicate where the extensions of the relevant terms, as I use them, overlap. See Christen et al. 2014, Church 2016, Hazlett 2012, Johnson 2017, Kidd 2016, Leary et al. 2017, Meagher et al. 2015, Spiegel 2012, Tanesini 2016b, and Whitcomb et al. 2015.

13. J. Dewey 1986, 136.

14. J. Dewey 1986, 136.

15. Brinson 2016.

16. Brinson 2016.

17. J. Dewey 1998, 105.

18. J. Dewey 2012, 101.

19. The phrase is not Dewey's; the idea of a "space of reasons" is borrowed from another American philosopher of the mid-twentieth century, Wilfrid Sellars. The view of democracy embraced in the text owes much to John Rawls and Jürgen Habermas.

20. Lynch 2012a.

21. See Lynch 2018.

22. J. Dewey (1927) 2016, 224. Dewey's point here, which I develop in the text, aligns with that made by Lee McIntyre (2019).

23. Plato 1992, 232, sec. 561 d.

24. Gawande 2010.

25. Rorty 2000, 2.

26. Leibniz 1996, 397–98.

27. Lynch 2009.

References and Additional Sources

Alcoff, Linda Martín. 2007. "Fraser on Redistribution, Recognition, and Identity." *European Journal of Political Theory* 6 (3): 255–65.

Arendt, Hannah. 1966. *The Origins of Totalitarianism*. New York: Harcourt.

Arendt, Hannah. 2006. *Between Past and Future: Eight Excercises in Political Thought*. New York: Penguin.

Baldwin, Dare A., Ellen M. Markman, and Rikkaa L. Melartin. 1993. "Infants' Ability to Draw Inferences about Nonobvious Object Properties: Evidence from Exploratory Play." *Child Development* 64 (3): 711–28.

Banaji, Mahzarin R. 2002. "Social Psychology of Stereotypes." In *International Encyclopedia of the Social and Behavioral Sciences*, edited by Neil J. Smelser and Paul B. Baltes, 15100–104. New York: Pergamon.

Bar-On, D., and M. Chrisman. 2009. "Ethical Neo-expressivism." In *Oxford Studies in Metaethics*, vol. 4, edited by Russ Shafer-Landau, 132–65. Oxford: Oxford University Press.

Battaly, Heather. 2018a. "Can Closed-Mindedness Be an Intellectual Vice?" *Royal Institute of Philosophy Supplement* 84: 23–45.

———. 2018b. "Closed-Mindedness and Dogmatism." *Episteme* 15 (special issue 3): 261–82.

Beavers, Olivia. 2017. "GOP Lawmaker Spars with CNN Reporter over Charlottesville Conspiracy Theories." *Hill*, October 26, 2017.

Bell, Macalester. 2013. *Hard Feelings: The Moral Psychology of Contempt* (Oxford: Oxford University Press).

Black, Derek. 2016. "Why I Left White Nationalism." *New York Times*, November 26, 2016.

Blackburn, Simon. 1998. *Ruling Passions: A Theory of Practical Reasoning*. Oxford: Clarendon Press.

Brady, William J., Julian A. Wills, John T. Jost, Joshua A. Tucker, and Jay J. Van Bavel. 2017. "Emotion Shapes the Diffusion of Moralized Content in Social Networks." *Proceedings of the National Academy of Sciences of the USA* 114 (28): 7313–18.

Brinson, Will. 2016. "Here's How Nate Boyer Got Colin Kaepernick to Go from Sitting to Kneeling." *CBS Sports*, September 27, 2016.

Camus, Albert. 1956. *The Rebel*. Translated by Anthony Bower. New York: Random House.

Chrisman, Matthew. 2008. "Expressivism, Inferentialism, and Saving the Debate." *Philosophy and Phenomenological Research* 77 (2): 334–58.

Christen, Markus, Mark Alfano, and Brian Robinson. 2014. "The Semantic Neighborhood of Intellectual Humility." In *Proceedings of the European Conference on Social Intelligence (ECSI-2014), Barcelona, Spain, November 3–5, 2014*, edited by Andreas Herzig and Emiliano Lorini, 40–49. CEUR-WS.org.

Church, Ian M. 2016. "The Doxastic Account of Intellectual Humility." *Logos and Episteme* 7 (4): 413–33.

Cohen, Geoffrey L. 2003. "Party over Policy: The Dominating Impact of Group Influence on Political Beliefs." *Journal of Personality and Social Psychology* 85: 808–22.

Cohen, Patricia. 2008. "Professor's Liberalism Contagious? Maybe Not," *New York Times*, November 3, 2008, https://www.nytimes.com/2008/11/03/books/03infl.html.

Crockett, Molly J. 2017. "Moral Outrage in the Digital Age." *Nature Human Behaviour* 1: 769–71.

———. 2018. "Modern Outrage Is Making It Harder to Better Society." *Globe and Mail*, March 2, 2018.

Dana, Jason, and George Loewenstein. 2003. "A Social Science Perspective on Gifts to Physicians from Industry." *Journal of the American Medical Association* 290: 252–55.

Darwall, Stephen L. 2006. *The Second-Person Standpoint: Morality, Respect, and Accountability*. Cambridge, MA: Harvard University Press.

———. 2013. *Honor, History, and Relationship: Essays in Second-Personal Ethics II*. Oxford: Oxford University Press.

Davidson, Donald. 2005. "The Socratic Concept of Truth." In *Truth, Language, and History*, 241–50. Oxford: Clarendon Press.

Dennett, Daniel C. 2014. "The Self as the Center of Narrative Gravity." In *Self and Consciousness: Multiple Perspectives*, edited by Frank S. Kessel, Pamela M. Cole, and Dale L. Johnson, 111–23. New York: Psychology Press.

Desan, Philippe. 2017. *Montaigne: A Life*. Translated by Steven Rendall and Lisa Neal. Princeton, NJ: Princeton University Press.

Dewey, Caitlin. 2016. "6 in 10 of You Will Share This Article without Reading It, a New Depressing Study Says." *Washington Post*, June 16, 2016.

Dewey, John. (1927) 2016. *The Public and Its Problems: An Essay in Political Inquiry*. Athens, OH: Swallow Press.

———. 1981. "Creative Democracy: The Task before Us." In *The Later Works of John Dewey, 1925–1953*, edited by J. A. Boydston, vol. 14, *1939–1941: Essays, Reviews, and Miscellany*, 224–30. Carbondale: Southern Illinois University Press, 1981.

———. 1986. *The Later Works: 1925–1953*, vol. 8. Carbondale: Southern Illinois University Press.

———. 1998. "The Problem of Truth." In *The Essential Dewey*, edited by Larry A. Hickman and Thomas M. Alexander, vol. 2, *Ethics, Logic, Psychology*, 101–30. Bloomington: Indiana University Press.

————. 2012. *Democracy and Education*. New York: Start Publishing.

Dillon, Robin S. 2003. "Kant on Arrogance and Self-Respect." In *Setting the Moral Compass: Essays by Women Philosophers*, edited by Chesire Calhoun, 191–216. Oxford: Oxford University Press.

————. 2015. "Humility, Arrogance, and Self-Respect in Kant and Hill." In *Reason, Value, and Respect: Kantian Themes from the Philosophy of Thomas E. Hill, Jr.*, edited by Mark Timmons and Robert N. Johnson, 42–69. New York: Oxford University Press.

Dovidio, John F., and Samuel L. Gaertner. 1991. "Changes in the Expression and Assessment of Racial Prejudice." In *Opening Doors: Perspectives of Race Relations in Contemporary America*, edited by Harry J. Knopke, Robert J. Norrell, and Ronald W. Rogers, 119–48. Tuscaloosa: University of Alabama Press.

————. 2004. "Aversive Racism." In *Advances in Experimental Social Psychology*, vol. 36, edited by Mark P. Zanna, 1–52. San Diego, CA: Academic Press.

Dunlap, Riley E., and Aaron M. McCright. 2008. "A Widening Gap: Republican and Democratic Views on Climate Change." *Environment: Science and Policy for Sustainable Development* 50 (5): 26–35.

Dunning, David. 2011. "The Dunning-Kruger Effect: On Being Ignorant of One's Own Ignorance." *Advances in Experimental Social Psychology* 44: 247–96.

Dunton, Bridget C., and Russell H. Fazio. 1997. "An Individual Difference Measure of Motivation to Control Prejudiced Reactions." *Personality and Social Psychology Bulletin* 23: 316–26.

Emerson, Ralph Waldo. 2000. *The Essential Writings of Ralph Waldo Emerson*, edited by Brooks Atkinson. New York: Modern Library.

Epley, Nicholas. 2015. *Mindwise: Why We Misunderstand What Others Think, Believe, Feel and Want*. New York: Vintage Books.

Epley, Nicholas, and David Dunning. 2000. "Feeling 'Holier than Thou': Are Self-Serving Assessments Produced by Errors in Self- or Social Prediction?" *Journal of Personality and Social Psychology* 79 (6): 861–75.

Fandos, Nicholas, and Kevin Roose. 2018. "Facebook Identifies an Active Political Influence Campaign Using Fake Accounts." *New York Times*, July 13, 2018.

Farhi, Paul. 2016. "False Flag Planted at a Pizza Place?" *Washington Post*, December 5, 2016.

Fazio, Russell H., Joni R. Jackson, Bridget C. Dunton, and Carol J. Williams. 1995. "Variability in Automatic Activation as an Unobtrusive Measure of Racial Attitudes: A Bona Fide Pipeline?" *Journal of Personality and Social Psychology* 69 (6): 1013–27.

Fingerhut, Hannah. 2017. "Republicans Skeptical of Colleges' Impact on U.S., but Most See Benefits for Workforce Preparation." Pew Research Center, July 20, 2017.

Fisher, Matthew, Mariel K. Goddu, and Frank C. Keil. 2015. "Searching for Explanations: How the Internet Inflates Estimates of Internal Knowledge." *Journal of Experimental Psychology* 144 (3): 674–87.

Flanagan, Owen. 1996. *Self Expressions: Mind, Morals, and the Meaning of Life.* New York: Oxford University Press.

Frank, Thomas. 2016. *Listen, Liberal: Or, What Ever Happened to the Party of the People?* New York: Metropolitan Books.

Frankfurt, Harry. 1988. *The Importance of What We Care About.* Cambridge: Cambridge University Press.

Fraser, Nancy. 2000. "Rethinking Recognition." *New Left Review*, May–June 2000.

Fricker, Miranda. 2007. *Epistemic Injustice: Power and the Ethics of Knowing.* Oxford: Oxford University Press.

Frost-Arnold, Karen. 2018. "Who Should We Be Online? A Social Epistemology for the Internet." Unpublished manuscript.

Gabielkov, Maksym, Arthi Ramachandran, Augustin Chaintreau, and Arnaud Legout. 2016. "Social Clicks: What and Who Gets Read on Twitter?" Paper presented at the ACM SIGMETRICS/IFIP Performance 2016, Antibes Juan-les-Pins, France, June 14, 2016.

Galinsky, Adam D., and Gordon B. Moskowitz. 2000. "Perspective-Taking: Decreasing Stereotype Expression, Stereotype Accessibility, and In-Group Favoritism." *Journal of Personality and Social Psychology* 78 (4): 708–24.

Gawande, Atul. 2010. *The Checklist Manifesto: How to Get Things Right.* New York: Metropolitan Books.

Gendler, Tamar Szabó. 2011. "On the Epistemic Costs of Implicit Bias." *Philosophical Studies* 156: 33–63.

Goldberg, Jonah. 2018. *Suicide of the West: How the Rebirth of Tribalism, Populism, Nationalism, and Identity Politics Is Destroying American Democracy.* New York: Crown Forum.

Goldberg, Sanford. 2010. *Relying on Others.* Oxford: Oxford University Press.

Goldman, Adam. 2016. "The Comet Ping Pong Gunman Answers Our Reporter's Questions." *New York Times,* December 7, 2016.

Gordon, Lewis R. 1995. *Bad Faith and Antiblack Racism.* Atlantic Highlands, NJ: Humanity Books.

———. 2000. "Racism as a Form of Bad Faith." *APA Newsletter on Philosophy and the Black Experience* 99 (2).

———. 2016. *Disciplinary Decadence: Living Thought in Trying Times.* London: Routledge.

Greene, Joshua. 2014. *Moral Tribes: Emotion, Reason, and the Gap between Us and Them.* New York: Penguin Group.

Greenwald, Anthony G., Debbie E. McGhee, and Jordan L. K. Schwartz. 1998. "Measuring Individual Differences in Implicit Cognition: The Implicit Association Test." *Journal of Personality and Social Psychology* 74 (6): 1464–80.

Grim, Ryan. 2016. "Nate Silver Is Unskewing Polls—All of Them—in Trump's Direction." HuffPost, November 5, 2016. https://www.huffingtonpost.com/entry/nate-silver-election-forecast_us_581e1c33e4b0d9ce6fbc6f7f.

Gunn, Hanna Kiri, and Michael P. Lynch. 2019. "Googling." In *The Routledge Handbook of Applied Epistemology,* edited by David Coady and James Chase, 41–53. New York: Routledge.

Harding, Sandra. 1991. *Whose Science? Whose Knowledge?: Thinking from Women's Lives.* Ithaca, NY: Cornell University Press.

———. 1993. "Rethinking Standpoint Epistemology: What Is 'Strong Objectivity'?" In *Feminist Epistemologies*, edited by Linda Alcoff and Elizabeth Potter, 49–82. Thinking Gender. New York: Routledge.

Haslanger, Sally. 2014. *Resisting Reality: Social Construction and Social Critique*. New York: Oxford University Press.

Hazlett, Allan. 2012. "Higher-Order Epistemic Attitudes and Intellectual Humility." *Episteme* 9 (3): 205–23.

Heath, Chip. 1999. "On the Social Psychology of Agency Relationships: Lay Theories of Motivation Overemphasize Extrinsic Incentives." *Organizational Behavior and Human Decision Processes* 78: 25–62.

Hendricks, Robert. 2010. *Lao-tzu: Te-tao ching: A New Translation Based on the Recently Discovered Ma-wang tui Texts* (New York: Ballantine Books).

Hochschild, Arlie Russell. 2018. *Strangers in Their Own Land: Anger and Mourning on the American Right*. New York: New Press.

Hume, David. (1888) 1978. *A Treatise of Human Nature*. Edited by P. H. Nidditch. Oxford: Oxford University Press.

———. 1999. *An Enquiry concerning Human Understanding*. Oxford: Oxford University Press.

Jaschik, Scott. 2016. "Professors, Politics, and New England." *Inside Higher Ed*, July 5, 2016.

———. 2017. "Professors, Politics: What the Research Says." *Inside Higher Ed*, February 27, 2017.

Johnson, Casey Rebecca. 2017. "Intellectual Humility and Empathy by Analogy." *Topoi*, 2017, 1–8.

Jost, John. 2015. "Resistance to Change: A Social Psychological Perspective." *Social Research* 81 (3): 607–36.

Kahan, Dan M. 2013. "Ideology, Motivated Reasoning, and Cognitive Reflection: An Experimental Study." *Judgment and Decision Making* 8 (4): 407–24.

Kahan, Dan M., Donald Braman, John Gastil, Paul Slovic, and C. K. Mertz. 2007. "Culture and Identity-Protective Cognition: Explaining the White-Male Effect in Risk Perception." *Journal of Empirical Legal Studies* 4 (3): 465–505.

Kahan, Dan M., Ellen Peters, Maggie Wittlin, Paul Slovic, Lisa Larrimore Ouellette, Donald Braman, and Gregory N. Mandel. 2012. "The Polarizing Impact of Science Literacy and Numeracy on Perceived Climate Change Risks." *Nature Climate Change* 2 (10): 732–35.

Kahneman, Daniel. 2011. *Thinking, Fast and Slow*. New York: Farrar, Straus and Giroux.

Keil, Frank C., Courtney Stein, Lisa Webb, Van Dyke Billings, and Leonid Rozenblit. 2008. "Discerning the Division of Cognitive Labor: An Emerging Understanding of How Knowledge Is Clustered in Other Minds." *Cognitive Science* 32 (2): 259–300.

Kidd, Ian James. 2016. "Intellectual Humility, Confidence, and Argumentation." *Topoi* 35 (2): 395–402.

———. 2018. "Epistemic Corruption and Education." *Episteme*, March 21, 2018, 1–16. https://doi.org/10.1017/epi.2018.3.

Kitcher, Philip. 1990. "The Division of Cognitive Labor." *Journal of Philosophy* 87 (1): 5–22.

Kornblith, Hilary. 2012. *On Reflection*. Oxford: Oxford University Press.

Leary, M. R., K. J. Diebels, E. K. Davisson, K. P. Jongman-Sereno, J. C. Isherwood, K. T. Raimi, S. A. Deffler, and R. H. Hoyle. 2017. "Cognitive and Interpersonal Features of Intellectual Humility." *Personality and Social Psychology Bulletin* 43 (6): 793–813.

Leibniz, Gottfried Wilhelm. 1996. *New Essays on Human Understanding*. Abridged ed. Translated and edited by Peter Remnant and Jonathan Bennett. Cambridge: Cambridge University Press.

Leslie, Sarah-Jane. 2017. "The Original Sin of Cognition: Fear, Prejudice, and Generalization." *Journal of Philosophy* 118 (8): 393–421.

Lilla, Mark. 2017. *The Once and Future Liberal: After Identity Politics*. New York: HarperCollins.

Lippmann, Walter. 1955. *The Public Philosophy*. New York: Mentor.

Lukianoff, Greg, and Jonathan Haidt. 2018. *The Coddling of the American Mind: How Good Intention and Bad Ideas Are Setting Up a Generation for Failure*. New York: Penguin.

Lynch, Michael P. 1998. *Truth in Context*. Cambridge, MA: MIT Press.

———. 2009. *Truth as One and Many*. Oxford: Oxford University Press.

———. 2012a. "Democracy as a Space of Reasons." In *Truth and Democracy*, edited by Jeremy Norris and Andrew Elkins, 114–29. Philadelphia: University of Pennsylvania Press.

———. 2012b. *In Praise of Reason: Why Rationality Matters for Democracy*. Cambridge, MA: MIT Press.

———. 2016. *The Internet of Us: Knowing More and Understanding Less in the Age of Big Data*. New York: Liveright Press.

———. 2018. "Academic Freedom and the Politics of Truth." In *Academic Freedom*, edited by J. Lackey, 23–35. Engaging Philosophy. Oxford: Oxford University Press.

MacIntyre, Alasdair. 1984. *After Virtue: A Study in Moral Theory*. 2nd ed. Notre Dame, IN: University of Notre Dame Press.

Manne, Kate. 2018. *Down Girl: The Logic of Misogyny*. New York: Oxford University Press.

McCright, Aaron M., and Riley E. Dunlap. 2011. "The Politicization of Climate Change and Polarization in the American Public's Views of Global Warming, 2001–2010." *Sociological Quarterly* 52 (2): 155–94.

McIntyre, Lee. *The Scientific Attitude: Defending Science from Denial, Fraud, and Pseudoscience*. Cambridge, MA: MIT Press, 2019.

Meagher, Benjamin R., Joseph C. Leman, Joshua P. Bias, Shawn J. Latendresse, and Wade C. Rowatt. 2015. "Contrasting Self-Report and Consensus Ratings of Intellectual Humility and Arrogance." *Journal of Research in Personality* 58: 35–45.

Meckler, Laura. 2018. "How Speaker Paul Ryan Warns against Identity Politics." *Wall Street Journal*, April 15, 2018.

Medina, José. 2012. *The Epistemology of Resistance: Gender and Racial Oppression, Epistemic Injustice, and the Social Imagination*. New York: Oxford University Press.

Menand, Louis. 2001–2. "Morton, Agassiz, and the Origins of Scientific Racism in the United States." *Journal of Blacks in Higher Education*, no. 34 (Winter 2001–2): 110–13.

Miller, Dale T., and Rebecca K. Ratner. 1998. "The Disparity between the Actual and Assumed Power of Self-Interest." *Journal of Personality and Social Psychology* 74 (1): 53–62.

Millikan, Ruth G. 2017. *Beyond Concepts: Unicepts, Language, and Natural Information.* Oxford: Oxford University Press.

Mills, Charles W. 1997. *The Racial Contract.* Ithaca, NY: Cornell University Press.

Montaigne, Michel de. 2003. *The Complete Essays.* Translated and edited by M. A. Screech. London: Penguin.

Mutz, Diana C. 2018. "Status Threat, Not Economic Hardship, Explains the 2016 Presidential Vote." *Proceedings of the National Academy of Sciences of the USA* 115 (19): E4330–39. https://doi.org/10.1073/pnas.1718155115.

Nietzsche, Friedrich. 2005. *Nietzsche: The Anti-Christ, Ecce Homo, Twilight of the Idols, and Other Writings.* Edited by Aaron Ridley and Judith Norman. Cambridge: Cambridge University Press.

Nordell, Jessica. 2017. "Is This How Discrimination Ends?" *Atlantic,* May 7, 2017.

Oakeshott, Michael. 1991. *Rationalism in Politics and Other Essays.* Indianapolis, IN: Liberty Fund.

Paul, L. A. 2014. *Transformative Experience.* Oxford: Oxford University Press.

Payne, B. Keith. 2001. "Prejudice and Perception: The Role of Automatic and Controlled Processes in Misperceiving a Weapon." *Journal of Personality and Social Psychology* 81 (2): 181–92.

Pew Research Center. 2009. "Public Praises Science; Scientists Fault Public, Media." July 9, 2009. http://www.people-press.org/2009/07/09/public-praises-science-scientists-fault-public-media.

———. 2016. "Partisan and Political Animosity in 2016." June 22, 2016. http://www.people-press.org/2016/06/22/partisanship-and-political-animosity-in-2016.

———. 2017. "The Partisan Divide on Political Values Grows Even Wider." October 5, 2017. http://www.people-press.org/2017/10/05/the-partisan-divide-on-political-values-grows-even-wider.

Pianalto, Matthew. 2011. "Moral Conviction." *Journal of Applied Philosophy* 28 (4): 381–95.

Pitkin, Hanna Fenichel. 1972. *Wittgenstein and Justice*. Berkeley: University of California Press.

Plato. 1928a. *Apology*, in *The Works of Plato*. Translated by B. Jowett. Edited by I. Edman. New York: Modern Library/Simon and Schuster. p. 486.

———. 1928b. *Theaetetus*, in *The Works of Plato*. Translated by B. Jowett. Edited by I. Edman. New York: Modern Library/Simon and Schuster. p. 486.

———. 1992. *The Republic*. Translated by G. M. A. Grube and C. D. C. Reeve. Indianapolis, IN: Hackett.

Pohlhaus, Gaile, Jr. 2012. "Relational Knowing and Epistemic Injustice: Toward a Theory of *Willful Hermeneutical Ignorance*." *Hypatia* 27 (4): 715–35.

Pronin, Emily, Jonah A. Berger, and Sarah Molouki. 2007. "Alone in a Crowd of Sheep: Asymmetric Perceptions of Conformity and Their Roots in an Introspection Illusion." *Journal of Personality and Social Psychology* 92 (4): 585–95.

Rawls, John. 1996. *Political Liberalism*. New York: Columbia University Press.

Reeve, Elspeth. 2017. "Congressman Suggests Charlottesville Was George Soros-Backed Conspiracy." *Vice News*, October 5, 2017.

Reilly, Katie. 2016. "Read Hillary Clinton's 'Basket of Deplorables' Remarks about Donald Trump Supporters." *Time*, September 10, 2016. http://time.com/4486502/hillary-clinton-basket-of-deplorables -transcript.

Rensin, Emmett. 2016. "The Smug Style in American Liberalism." *Vox*, April 21, 2016.

Ricks, Thomas E. 2006. *Fiasco: The American Military Adventure in Iraq*. New York: Penguin.

Ridge, Michael. 2014. *Impassioned Belief*. Oxford: Oxford University Press.

Rini, Regina. 2017. "Fake News and Partisan Epistemology." *Kennedy Institute of Ethics Journal* 27: 43–64.

Robinson, Robert J., Dacher Keltner, Andrew Ward, and Lee Ross. 1995. "Actual versus Assumed Differences in Construal: 'Naïve Realism' in Intergroup Perception and Conflict." *Journal of Personality and Social Psychology* 68 (3): 404–17.

Rorty, Richard. 1979. *Philosophy and the Mirror of Nature.* Princeton, NJ: Princeton University Press.

———. 2000. "Universality and Truth." In *Rorty and His Critics,* edited by Robert B. Brandom, 1–30. Cambridge: Blackwell.

Rozenblit, Leonid, and Frank Keil. 2002. "The Misunderstood Limits of Folk Science: An Illusion of Explanatory Depth." *Cognitive Science* 26: 521–62.

Russell, Bertrand. *Sceptical Essays.* London: George Allen & Unwin, 1935.

Saslow, Eli. 2016. "The White Flight of Derek Black." *Washington Post,* October 15, 2016.

Schmitt, Carl. 2008. *The Concept of the Political.* Expanded ed. Translated and edited by G. Schwab. Chicago: University of Chicago Press.

Schroeder, Mark. 2008. *Being For.* Oxford: Oxford University Press.

Sharockman, Aaron. 2017. "Infowars' Alex Jones Falsely Says George Soros, Hillary Clinton Instigated Charlottesville Violence." *Politifact,* August 14, 2017.

Skitka, Linda J., Christopher W. Bauman, and Edward G. Sargis. 2005. "Moral Conviction: Another Contributor to Attitude Strength or Something More?" *Journal of Personality and Social Psychology* 88 (6): 895–917.

Sloman, Steven, and Philip Fernbach. 2017. *The Knowledge Illusion: Why We Never Think Alone.* New York: Riverhead Books.

Smith, Mychal Denzel. 2017. "What Liberals Get Wrong about Identity Politics." *New Republic,* September 11, 2017.

Snyder, Timothy. 2015. *Black Earth: The Holocaust as History and Warning.* New York: Tim Duggan Books.

Spiegel, James S. 2012. "Open-Mindedness and Intellectual Humility." *School Field* 10 (1): 27–38.

Stanley, Jason. 2015. *How Propoganda Works.* Princeton, NJ: Princeton University Press.

———. 2018. *How Fascism Works: The Politics of Us and Them*. New York: Random House.

Strang, Stephen E. 2017. *God and Donald Trump*. Lake Mary, FL: Charisma House Book Group.

Talisse, Robert B. 2009. *Democracy and Moral Conflict*. New York: Cambridge University Press.

———. Forthcoming. *Overdoing Democracy: Why We Must Put Politics in Its Place*. Oxford: Oxford University Press.

Tanesini, Alessandra, ed. 1999. *An Introduction to Feminist Epistemologies*. Malden, MA: Blackwell.

———. 2016a. "'Calm Down, Dear': Intellectual Arrogance, Silencing and Ignorance." *Aristotelian Society Supplementary Volume* 90 (1): 71–92.

———. 2016b. "Intellectual Humility as an Attitude." *Philosophy and Phenomenological Research* 96 (2): 399–420.

Taylor, Charles. 1994. *Multiculturalism: Examining the Politics of Recognition*. Edited by Amy Gutmann. Princeton, NJ: Princeton University Press.

Uhlmann, Eric Luis, and Geoffrey L. Cohen. 2007. "'I Think It, Therefore It's True': Effects of Self-Perceived Objectivity on Hiring Discrimination." *Organizational Behavior and Human Decision Process* 104: 207–23.

Vivian, James E., and Norman H. Berkowitz. 1992. "Anticipated Bias from an Outgroup: An Attributional Analysis." *European Journal of Social Psychology* 22: 415–24.

Walzer, Michael. 2006. *Politics and Passion: Toward a More Egalitarian Liberalism*. New Haven, CT: Yale University Press.

Whitcomb, Dennis, Heather Battaly, Jason Baher, and Daniel Howard-Snyder. 2015. "Intellectual Humility: Owning Our Limitations." *Philosophy and Phenomenological Research* 91 (1).

Williams, Bernard. 1985. *Ethics and the Limits of Philosophy*. Cambridge, MA: Harvard University Press.

Wittgenstein, Ludwig. 1969. *On Certainty*. Oxford: Basil Blackwell, 1969.

Index

Page numbers beginning with 173 refer to endnotes.

abortion, 79
action, 53
  beliefs and, 5, 8
  choice of, 7
  cognitive, 16
  commitment to, 55
  communicative, 39–40
  convictions and, 6, 53, 55
  drastic, 10
  expressive, 40
  intellectual arrogance in, 39
  lack of, 14
  thought and, 5
ACT UP, 153
affection, 42
Agassiz, Louis, 70
agreement, 156, 164, 165, 167
AIDS, 153
Alcoff, Linda, 180
algorithms, 29
Alt-Right, 120, 131, 132
American dream, 90
anger, 91, 122, 131, 133, 135, 138

anti-Semitism, 31, 94, 108
anxiety, 51, 78, 90, 92, 100, 129
apocalypse, 10
apologies, 44, 82
Arendt, Hannah, 4, 75–76, 78–79,
  92, 93, 98–99, 101, 155
Aristophanes, 142
Aristotle, 81, 153
arrogance, 36, 53, 74, 79, 86, 138,
  141
  attractiveness of, 77–78
  beliefs and, 2–3, 12
  combating of, 8, 151, 159
  confidence vs., 78
  conviction giving rise to, 6
  dogmatic, 3
  intellectual, 2–3, 6, 12, 13, 14,
    20–26, 39, 95, 97, 98, 141–42,
    153, 158, 160, 165, 175
  liberal, 121, 123, 193–94
  moral, 2
  political, 2–3, 5
  seeds of, 14, 21

arrogance (*continued*)
  as social failing, 6, 25–26
  tendency toward, 11, 12, 36
  tribal, 6, 25–26, 36, 92, 93, 95–96,
    97, 152, 162, 163, 170
  warnings about, 12, 100, 142
  about worldview, 6, 10, 12, 21–23,
    52, 98, 149
art, 145
Aryan culture, 77
Asia, 142
aspiration, 6, 55, 56–57, 110
assumptions, 143
atheism, 25
Athens, 142, 153
attitudes, 55, 58, 73, 137
  adoption of, 13
  change of, 5, 63–64, 126
  definition of, 5
  disavowal of, 5
  emotional, 43, 46
  inquiring, 149
  open-minded vs. closed-minded,
    34, 51, 62, 100, 131, 150, 151
  polarized, 12
  post-truth, 163–64
  reinforcement of, 77
  relationships and, 5
  sharing of, 7, 46
  skeptical, 9
  social, 18–26
  transitory, 26
  toward truth and evidence, 37
  unforgiving, 31–32
  validation of, 82
Austria, 4
authoritarianism, 75–79, 92, 99, 130
autism, 3

Bar-On, Dorit, 176
basketball, 42, 46
Battaly, Heather, 176, 179
beliefs, 141, 143
  action and, 5, 8
  arrogance about, 2–3, 12

biased, 17–18, 30
changing of, 5
confidence about, 20
in conspiracy theories, 39
convictions and, 61, 68–74, 93
dogmatic, 2, 4–5
entrenched, 164
false, 7, 33
forcible promotion of, 136
forming of, 1–2, 3, 4, 5, 8, 16–18,
  46, 144
foundational, 148
groundlessness of, 53
moral, 144
political, 144
protest and, 5
reinforcement of, 29–30
religious, 10, 25, 60
tribal, 3, 4, 7
truth of, 165, 168
uncertainty over, 10, 34
value of, 5
Bell, Macalester, 181
Bennett, Bill, 117–18
bias, 30, 142
  confirmation of, 34
  correcting for, 41, 158
  implicit, 17–18, 160
  information tailored to, 32
Birmingham, Ala., 153
Black, Derek, 147–48
Black Lives Matter, 112
Bloom, Alan, 117–18
Bolsheviks, 31
Bordeaux, 11
Boyer, Mark, 154
Boy Scouts of America, 81
brain function, 74
Brazil, 4
Breitbart, 132
Brooks, Arthur, 93
Brooks, David, 93, 125
bullying, 138
Burke, Edmund, 124
Butler, Judith, 125

INDEX

Cambridge Analytica, 32
Camus, Albert, 3
cell phones, 28
censorship, 100
certainty:
  desire for, 12
  moral, 2
change:
  of attitudes, 5, 63–64, 126
  of beliefs, 5
  cultural and demographic, 12
  fear of, 7
  resistance to, 53
  social, 14
charisma, 35
Charisma Media, 80
Charlottesville, Va., 94, 131, 132, 133
Checklist Manifesto, The (Gawande), 158
checklists, 158–60
children, 25, 55, 58, 75, 78, 103, 146
  alleged sex-trafficking of, 30–31, 37–38
  birth of, 113–14
  raising of, 4, 137
  welfare of, 56
Christianity, 90
  evangelical, 79–81, 84–85
  values of, 79, 84, 88
civility, 5, 12, 24, 133
civilization, end of, 10
civil rights movement, 38, 60, 107, 153
Civil War, U.S., 94–97
  monuments of, 94, 95, 96–97
climate change, 3, 63–68, 70–71,
  101, 162
Clinton, Hillary:
  conspiracy theories about, 30–31,
  37–38, 40
  "deplorables" remark of, 85, 178
  2016 presidential campaign of, 121
Clouds, The (Aristophanes), 142
CNN, 96
Colson, Chuck, 84
Columbia University, 41
Combahee River Collective, 106–7,
  109, 112, 114, 180

commitments, 56, 61, 69
  to action, 55
  adoption of, 74
  challenge of, 51
  emotional, 53
  moral, 69
communication:
  active, 39–40
  distraction by, 43
  moral, 45
  online, 39–42, 46, 47–48
  primary function of, 42–43, 46
  verbal, 35, 37, 39–40, 44
communitarianism, 113
communities, 113, 125
competence, 15
concepts, 145–47
  discourse on, 146–47
  stretching of, 146
Confederacy, 95
confidence, 2, 47, 78, 150
confusion, 33–34, 41, 44
con games, 33
Conservapedia, 103–4, 121
conservatives, 117–18, 123, 124,
  126–27, 129, 131
conspiracy theories, 30–31, 37–39,
  93–95, 132
  belief in, 39
  supported evidence for, 34–35
contempt, 130–38
convictions, 59–74, 83, 136, 177
  action and, 6, 53, 55
  arrogance and, 6
  aspiration and, 56–57
  attacks on, 6
  attitudes toward, 13–14
  belief and, 61, 68–74, 93
  blind, 7, 72, 73, 100
  certainty of, 54
  challenge of, 54
  changes in, 147–49
  confidence about, 7
  defending of, 62
  definitions of, 6, 57, 59

convictions (*continued*)
  emotional component of, 54
  expansion of, 7
  faulty, 143
  forming of, 1, 7, 54, 63, 91, 144
  having courage of, 51
  ignoring evidence against, 6
  loss of, 59
  maintaining of, 13, 14, 141
  moral, 13, 70, 71
  nature of, 53, 67
  opposition to, 54
  reason and, 8, 66
  reinforcement of, 7
  religious, 60
  of right and wrong, 13
  settled, 154
  testing of, 148
  tribal, 36
  about truth, 37
cooperation, 5
Copernicus, 10
corruption, 142, 162
  bribery and, 37
  of information culture, 37, 98
  pollution vs., 36–37
  protests of, 38
courage, 51
creation, 147
crime, 64, 81
Crockett, Molly, 42, 43–44
Cruz, Ted, 121
cynicism, 98
Czechoslovakia, 70

Darwall, Stephen, 181
death penalty, 44–45
death threats, 38
deception, 31–33
  intention and, 32–33
  lying vs., 32
  self-, 36, 37, 49
  sleight of hand and, 33
  as "success term," 33

defensiveness, 7, 23, 79, 95
deism, 123
democracy, 4, 11, 105, 109, 124, 125–26, 132, 134–36, 149, 155
  challenges of, 6
  citizens of, 157, 170
  convictions and ideals of, 14, 134
  fragility of, 54
  ideals of, 170
  liberal, 32
  value of truth in, 8
Democratic Party, 25, 30, 34, 58, 85, 86–87, 89, 121, 124, 128
Dennett, Daniel, 177
Descartes, René, 54, 61, 166
desire, 12, 68, 100
Dewey, John, 149, 150, 154–55, 156–58, 162
dialogue, 143–44, 147–48
Dickens, Charles, 57
Dillon, Robin, 181
discovery, 10, 128, 147
discrimination, 17–18, 37
dissent, 152–54, 161
doctors, 158, 159, 160
dogmatism, 3, 11, 53, 170
  religious, 10
  spread of, 4–5, 30
doom, prophecies of, 10
doubt, 54, 61, 153
Douthat, Ross, 93
Dunning, David, 15

Earth, 118, 151
  as center of the universe, 10
  circling of the sun by, 20
economic power structure, 85–86
ego, truth and, 23–24, 98–99, 143, 151
elections, 9
  presidential, 2, 3, 69, 80–92, 121–23
Emerson, Ralph Waldo, 53
emoji, 47–48

INDEX

emotions, 43, 54, 137
  building bonds of, 46, 47, 73,
    83–84
  conveying of, 40, 45–47, 49
  facial expression of, 47
  sharing of, 83–84
  tribal, 46
  see also passion; sentiments
enemies, 92, 108
Enlightenment, 105
enthusiasm, 53
esteem, signs of, 20
Europe, 10, 13, 70, 142
existence, 54, 61
existentialism, 56
experts, 22, 135
  questioning of, 27, 139, 140
expressivism, 45, 49

Facebook, 39, 72, 175–76
  advertisements on, 29
  emotional connections on, 47
fact-checking, 161
facts, 32, 62, 71
  "alternative," 3, 120
  citing of, 27, 83
  civic, 4
  contempt for, 79
  disagreement over, 12
  disregard of, 81, 83
  "hidden," 82, 83
  questioning of, 1
  sources of, 12
  teaching of, 4
fairness, 145
faith:
  bad, 99–100, 122, 130
  blind, 10, 72
  loss of, 59, 60
"fake news," 1, 3, 7, 24, 30–32, 36,
    134, 162
  accusations of, 39
  harm of, 31
  manipulation with, 32

for profit and political gain,
    31–32
  purveyors of, 44, 49
  susceptibility to, 34
"false flag attacks," 38, 94, 96
falsehoods, 30–35, 98
  belief in, 7, 33
  corruption and, 39
  distinguishing truth from, 52
  outrageous, 34–35
  pronouncement of, 3
family, 55, 60, 145
fascism, 76
fear, 121, 148
  of change, 7
  exploitation of, 7
  of ignorance, 21
  of mistakes, 23
  of status loss, 87–88, 92–93
feminism, 106–7, 112, 113
  black, 106
Fernbach, Phil, 174
Fiasco (Ricks), 22–23
figure skating, 146
Fisher, Matthew, 28
Florida, 147
Founding Fathers, 123
Fox News, 122, 128
France, sixteenth-century, 10–11
Frank, Thomas, 85
Franklin, Benjamin, 31
Fraser, Nancy, 112–13
free assembly, 156
freedom, 109, 132
free press, 156
free trade, 70
Freud, Sigmund, 5
Frost-Arnold, Karen, 176

Galileo Galilei, 20
games, 145–46
Gawande, Atul, 158, 160
gay marriage, 66, 79
genius, 24

INDEX

geography, 10, 76
globalism, 80
God, 84, 117
God and Donald Trump (Strang), 80–81
Godwin, Pearce, 131
Goebbels, Joseph, 132
Goldberg, Jonah, 93, 108–9, 127
Goldberg, Sandy, 176
goodness, 11
Google, ix, 27–30, 104
"Google-knowing," 27–28
Gordon, Lewis, 179
Gosar, Paul, 94
grammar, 15
Great Britain, 4, 31
greed, 79
Greek philosopy, 18, 19, 164, 165
    see also Socrates
grit, 19
groupthink, 123–24
guessing, 33, 91
guilt, 62
gun control legislation, 67
gun violence, 38, 63, 65, 132

Habermas, Jürgen, 124, 182
Haidt, Jonathan, 180
happiness, 11, 165–66
Harding, Sandra, 119
Harvard University, 127
Haslanger, Sally, 180
hatred, 11, 74, 77
health care, 101
hearts, 35
    and minds, 36
    power of, 45
Heyer, Heather, 94
Hitler, Adolf, 76–78
Hochschild, Arlie Russell, 58, 82, 90, 91
Hollywood, 128
Holocaust, 75, 76
hostility, 77, 163
hubris, 18–20

HuffPost, 121, 122
humanity, 76, 152
    nature of, 15
    observations about, 11
    quest for truth in, 9–10
    worst in, 26
human rights, 111
human welfare, 156
Hume, David, 5, 16–17, 18, 19–20, 44, 149
    character and personality of, 35
    critical insights of, 35–36, 45
humility, 14, 24, 151, 169
    lack of, 79
    necessity of, ix
    see also intellectual humility
Hungary, 4
hunger, 40
hurricanes, 63, 64
hypocrisy, 4

Icarus, 18, 19
idealism, 8
ideas, 150
    association of, 16–17
identity:
    family, 55, 105
    national, 58
    personal, 55, 56, 105
    political, 65
    social, 55, 56, 105, 109, 113
    tribal, 60
    see also self-identity
identity politics, 105–9, 120
    advocates of, 106
    critics of, 104–5, 106, 107, 108
    exercises in, 106
    two concepts of, 105–8, 112
ideology, 53, 74, 79, 100, 152, 162
    Nazi, 76–77
ignorance:
    admission of, 139, 149
    fear of, 21
"illusion of explanatory depth," 15, 28
immigration, 101, 145

INDEX

incivility, 6
infallibility, 3, 78
information, 73
   access to, 12, 28
   alternative, 34
   analysis of, 29
   bubbles of, 30, 34
   confirmation of, 20–30
   contradictory, 164
   conveying of, 36
   corrupted, 49
   deceptive, 31–33
   disagreement over, 12
   dismissal of, 35
   doubting of, 34
   false, 3, 4, 7, 30–35, 39
   misuse of, 30
   political use of, 30–31
   prediction of, 29
   processing of, 16
   recommendation and endorsement
      of, 40–41
   reliability of, 37
   sharing of, 37, 40–42
   sources of, 24–25, 27–30, 34, 35
   technological, 12
   testimonial, 40
   as tool of empire and war, 31
   toxic, 31
   vulnerability to, 49
   weaponizing of, 3
   word of mouth, 37
   see also "fake news"; news
information pollution, 7, 30–35, 36,
      39, 98, 100.170
   definition of, 31
   golden age of, 32
   justification of, 31
   political use of, 32
inquiry, 149, 157, 161, 163, 165, 166
intellectual elitism, 126, 128, 129
intellectual humility, 8, 51, 149–54,
      160, 182
   adopting of, 149, 150
   democracy and, 150

   encouragement of, 161
   essence of, 169
intelligence, 17, 69–70
internet, 106
   apps of, 29
   clicking on links on, 29, 41
   creation of, 36
   digital platforms on, 45–46
   know-it-all culture encouraged on, 35
   personalization of, 32
   political misinformation on, 33
   as reinforcement mechanism, 30
   search engines on, 27–30
   sharing content on, 39–42, 46
   shopping on, 32
   social platforms on, 3, 7, 9, 29, 32
   speed and ease of access to, 28
   spread of outrage on, 4
   videos and stories on, 37–38, 40
Internet of Things, 29
Internet of Us, 29
intuition, 16, 17, 21, 113
Iraq War, 22
irony, 21, 35, 40, 116, 154
Islamic terrorism, 80

jazz, 146
Johnson, Lyndon B., 23
Jones, Alex, 94
judgment:
   automatic and involuntary, 17
   biased, 17–18
   forming of, 17
   moral, 45
   rational and deliberate, 15–16
   removal of, 58
justice, 70, 141
   social, 170

Kaepernick, Colin, 152, 153–54
Kahan, Dan, 66–67, 68, 178
Kahneman, Daniel, 174
Kansas, 123
Kant, Immanuel, 110, 124, 134, 145
Kennedy, John F., 23

know-it-alls, 2, 162
    characteristics of, 21–26, 74, 86, 103
    internet encouragement of, 35
knowledge, 73, 78, 114
    common, 123, 174
    confusing power with, 142
    dialogue as path to, 143–44
    lack of, 33, 139–42, 143, 144
    overestimating of, 15–18, 21,
        28–30, 139
    pursuit of, 11, 143–44, 157
    of right vs. wrong, 52
    shared, 114–15
    transfer of, 43
    of unrelated subjects, 28
    wisdom vs., 140
Kristof, Nicholas, 127

language, 52, 92, 144
    expressive, 49
    hypocrisy and, 4
    moral, 44
    of symbols, 58
Lao-tzu, 142
Lee, Robert E., 94
legislation, 4
liberals, 103–5, 117, 125, 128–30, 138
    arrogance of, 121, 123, 193–94
    in higher education, 126–29
    traditional, 125
    values of, 104, 108
liberty, 145
light, speed of, 169
Lilla, Mark, 107–9
Listen First Project, 131
listening, 24, 150
Locke, John, 113, 124
logic, 52, 53, 54, 62, 65, 66, 119
Lorde, Audre, 106
loyalty, 75, 78, 82, 100
    truth and., 6
lying, 4, 32–33, 151
    deception vs., 32
    see also falsehoods

Machiavelli, Niccolò, 31, 108
Manne, Kate, 179
marriage, 115, 145, 146
Marx, Karl, 153
Marxism, 107, 112
Medina, José
memes, 105, 106
#MeToo movement, 114
military training, 46–47
Mill, John Stuart, 166
Millikan, Ruth, 176
Mills, Charles, 125
mind:
    change of, 51–53, 99
    empty, 150
    faculties of, 16
    frame of, see attitudes
    hearts and, 36
    mechanisms of, 17
    strength of, 20
mistakes, 15, 39
    admission of, 21, 78–79
    fear of, 23
money, 59, 85
Montaigne, Michel de, 9–16, 18, 149,
        166, 173
    Catholic faith of, 12
    influence of, 16
    political life of, 9, 10, 11
    skepticism of, 143
    teaching of, 26, 141–42
    works of, 9, 11
    on worldview, 6, 10, 12
moon landing conspiracy theories, 34
Moore, Russell, 84
morality, 44–45, 60, 69, 73–74,
        136–37
    communication of, 45
    sentiments of, 42
    social passion and, 36
Moses, 16
Muslims, 17, 89
Mutz, Diana, 86, 87, 88–89
myths, 18–19, 97

INDEX

national consciousness, 2
nationalism, 4, 76, 92, 93
  white, 147
National Socialist Party, 78
nature, 36
Nazis, 76–77, 94–95, 108, 131–32,
    151
  atrocities of, 156
  "Blood and Soil" slogan of, 94
  Stormfront website of, 147
negotiation, 146–47
neo-Nazis, 13, 94
news, 1, 161
  editing of, 34
  misleading, 31
  sharing of, 40–41, 43
  sources of, 35
  twenty-four-hour cycle of, 9
  see also "fake news"
New World, discovery of, 10
New York, N.Y., 80
New York Times, 06, 30, 147–48
Nietzsche, Friedrich, 62–63, 168
1984 (Orwell), 169–70
Niobe, 19
Noah, 16
North Carolina, 63

Oakeshott, Michael, 124–25
Obama, Barack, 80, 122
obligations, 60
obsessions, 8, 142
opinions, 118, 134
  agreement with, 20
  alternate, 24
  confidence in, 20
  political, 145
  shaping of, 17, 141
  shifting of, 52
  see also beliefs
oppression, 114
optimism, 125
Oracle of Delphi, 11
Orwell, George, 169

outrage, 42133
  moral, 43–44
overconfidence, 15, 19, 20, 30

Paine, Thomas, 153
partisanship, 150
passion, 54
  reason as slave of, 35, 36, 39
  role of, 36
  rousing of, 31
  social, 36
  social media as vehicle for, 30
peer pressure, 68
performance, self-rating of, 15
Pew Research Center, 126, 128
philosophy, ix, 5, 8, 16, 35, 167, 168
  Greek, 11, 142, 143, 165–66
  justification of, 52
  political, 124–25
  problems of, 13–14, 52
Pilate, Pontius, 167
pilots, 159, 160
Pizzagate conspiracy story, 30–31, 34,
    37–38, 94
Plato, 141, 142, 145, 157, 158
Pliny, 12
polemic, 3
police, 37
political correctness, 134
politics, 63–65
  abandonment of, 9, 14
  acquiring and maintaining convic-
    tions about, 1, 7
  agreement vs. disagreement on, 2
  arrogance in, 2–3, 5
  of contempt, 130–38
  current American, 79–84
  debates on, 146–47
  demonstrations in, 13
  disagreement in, 165
  discourse in, 3
  dogmatic, 13
  give and take in, 14
  identity, *see* identity politics

politics (*continued*)
  Left vs. Right, 1, 13, 38, 70, 79, 81,
    83, 85, 86, 93, 95, 107–9, 112,
    116, 119–20, 122, 127, 131, 138
  polarization in, 5, 7, 12
  purpose of, 108, 110
  rational argument in, 8
  recognition, 110
  suspicion and resentment in, 2, 14
  talking, 103
  tribal, 112, 114, 117
  truth in, 4
  upheaval in, 10
  war and, 108
pollution, 64
pornography, 146
postmodernism, 115
"post-truth" culture, 37, 163–64
power, 133, 141
  conflict with those in, 151
  desire for, 108
  of hearts, 45
  knowledge confused with, 142
  as measure of success, 3
  political, 78
  seizure of, 79
prediction, 78
prejudice, 125, 143, 150
  racist and sexist, 17–18, 69–70
  religious, 17, 31
  social, 17–18, 37
  stereotypes and, 17–18
pride, ix, 23, 104
progressivism, 103, 104, 116, 117,
    120, 129–30
Prometheus, 19
propaganda, 3, 7, 32, 33, 36, 71
prophecy, 10
Protagoras, 164
protest, 5, 38, 152, 153–54
  violent vs. nonviolent, 60, 161
Protestantism, 81
Protestant Reformation, 10
Protocols of the Elders of Zion, The, 31

psychology, social, 5
public debate, 64, 100, 146–47
public discourse, 156
Putin, Vladimir, 69
Pyrrhonian skeptics, 11, 12

QAnon, 31

racism, 17–18, 37, 59, 69–70, 76, 77,
    85, 88, 92, 115, 123, 131, 133,
    147–48, 152
rape, 115, 119
rationality, 8, 15–16, 67, 124–25
Rawls, John, 124, 182
reason, 124, 125, 129
  conviction and, 8, 66
  motivated, 17
  as slave of passion, 35, 36, 39
  sound, 18
recognition politics, 111–13, 119
reference, frames of, 52, 53
reflection, 16, 18, 24, 48, 49, 105,
    143, 148
  practices of, 158, 160–61
relations:
  attitudes and, 5
  interactive, 12
  personal, 3
relativism, 116–20, 164
religion, 10–13, 60, 116, 146
  belief in, 10, 25
  blind faith in, 10
  conflict and violence in, 10, 11
  extremism in, 10
  moral distinctions in, 36
  truth and, 10
  zealotry in, 13
renegotiation, 147, 154
Republic, The (Plato), 1, 141
Republican National Convention of
    2016, 81
Republican Party, 25, 58, 80, 94, 121,
    126, 128
"research" firms, 32

resentment, 77, 80, 90, 91
respect, 154, 156, 170
    equal, 11, 110
    mutual, 150
Ricks, Thomas, 22–23
righteousness, 137, 170
Rini, Regina, 176
Roman Catholic Church, 10, 12
Rorty, Richard, 116, 125, 165
Rousseau, Jean-Jacques, 124
Rubio, Marco, 121
Russell, Bertrand, ix, 8, 155
Russian Revolution, 31
Russian troll farms, 32, 33

Sanders, Bernie, 85
Sandy Hook Elementary School, 132
San Francisco 49ers, 152
Sartre, Jean-Paul, 56, 98
Schmitt, Carl, 108
science, 22, 64, 69, 83
    cognitive, 15, 74
    discoveries of, 10
    teaching of, 65, 66
Scruton, Roger, 125
self-assurance, 3, 7, 17, 47, 54
    social rewards of, 20
self-certainty, 8, 53
self-control, 19
self-esteem, 2, 20, 77, 95
    grit and, 19
    praise and, 19
self-expression, 45
self-identity, 56–60, 62, 71–72, 91,
        107, 148, 173
    aspirations and, 6, 110
    attacks on, 6
    formation of, 57–58, 66, 72, 83,
        111
    protection of, 7
    reinforcement of, 7, 83
self-image, 56
selfishness, 79, 107
Seneca Indians, 31

sentiments, 5, 17, 18, 59
    expression of, 40
    moral, 42
    of outrage, 4
sexism, 17, 85, 88, 115, 123, 135
sex-trafficking, 30–31, 37–38
shell game, 33
Silver, Nate, 121–22
skepticism, 9, 33, 61, 68, 118, 125,
        143, 150, 162, 163, 164
    Pyrrhonian, 11, 12
slavery, 95
sleight of hand, 33
Sloman, Steve, 174
Smith, Adam, 145
Smith, Barbara, 106
smoking, 56
Snyder, Timothy, 76
social constructions, 115–17
social hierarchies, collapse of, 111
social media, 32, 46, 49, 53, 72–73,
        100, 104, 136
    as a blind-conviction machine, 7, 73
    as boot camp for emotions, 47
    fake, 32
    information weaponized in, 3
    as an outrage factory, 44
    propaganda on, 33–34
    quitting of, 9
    sharing stories on, 40
    as a vehicle for passion, 39
societal rules, 37, 39, 43, 47
Socrates, 1, 3, 4, 8, 148–49, 151
    dialogues of, 139–41, 144
    elenchus method of, 139–43
    philosophy of, 142
    teaching of, 11, 149, 162
    trial and death sentence of, 140, 141,
        142
    value of dissent to, 152–53
Soros, George, 70, 94
Southern Baptist Church, 84
Soviet Union, 70
spaces of reason, 155, 156–57, 158, 163

INDEX

sports, 22
  Olympic, 146
Stalin, Joseph, 70
standpoint epistemology, 113–14, 119, 120
Stanley, Jason, 97, 132, 175
stars, 169
starvation, 115
stereotypes, 17–18, 174
Stevenson, Matthew, 147
Strang, Stephen, 79–81, 83–84, 86, 87, 92, 101
success, 142
  power as measure of, 3
"success terms," 33
suicide, 67
Suicide of the West (Goldberg), 108
sun, revolving of Earth around, 20
superiority:
  moral, 85, 97, 101
  sense of, 13, 25–26, 77, 78, 85, 97
suspicion, 2, 10
  political, 14

Talisse, Robert, 181
Tanesini, Alessandra, 175, 180, 182
Taylor, Charles, 180
"team-building," 46–47
technology, 36
  benefits of, 35
  information, 12
Theaetetus (Socrates), 139–41
Third Reich, *see* Nazis
thought, 155
  action and, 5
  associative, 21
  concerns about, 14
  critical, 124, 149
  existence and, 54, 61
  experiments with, 48, 49, 59, 133
  expression of, 144
  logical structure of, 52
  moral, 44
  reflective, 16, 18, 24, 48, 49, 105, 143, 148

sophisticated, 16
  unconscious and automatic, 16, 17
  see also groupthink; intuition
totalitarianism, 32, 75–76
transgender rights, 101, 110
tribes, 7, 60, 77, 112, 119, 173
  arrogance of, 6, 25–26, 78, 92, 93, 95–96, 97, 152, 162, 163, 170
  belief in infallibility of, 3, 4, 77
  betrayal of, 62
  bonding in, 42, 47, 82
  competition among, 76, 108
  emotional attitudes in, 46
  formation of, 43–44
  hierarchy of, 25
  loyalty of, 100, 106
  nationalism of, 92
  nature of, 58
  overconfidence about, 30
  politics of, 112, 114, 117
trolls, 32, 33, 44
Trump, Donald J., 39, 79–92, 131–33, 152
  administration of, 120, 128, 163
  character of, 121, 163
  "Make America Great Again" slogan of, 87, 89
  political support for, 79–81, 82, 84–88, 91–92
  presidential election of, 3, 69, 80–92, 121–23
  speeches of, 81–82
  Twitter rants of, 132, 177
  wealth of, 90
trust, 28
  break down of, 162
  building of, 46–47
  -self, 160
truth, ix, 33, 37, 78, 134, 163, 167
  access to, 157
  arrogant indifference to, 3, 4
  attitudes toward, 4, 100
  convictions about, 37
  "correspondence theory" of, 168

distinguishing falsehood from, 52
emotional, 82
equating ego with, 23–24, 98–99, 151
giving up quest for, 11
inadvertent, 33
nature of, 163–67
objective, 164
political, 4
politically important, 153
putting loyalty before, 6
quest for, 9–10, 11, 139, 143, 151,
    156–58, 166–67, 169
regard for, 36
relativism and, 116–20
religious, 10
self-deception and, 37
speaking, 81–82
substitution of lies for, 4
value of, 8, 155
Twitter, 39, 41, 42, 132, 177
tyrants, 162

unhappiness, Montaigne on, 11
United States, 4, 124
    "America First" attitude in, 89–90
    cultural and demographic change
        in, 12
    economy of, 88
    "exceptionalism" of, 89
    issue of border wall in, 13
    mass shootings in, 38, 63, 132
    presidential elections in, 2, 37,
        79–92, 121–23
universe, 169
    Earth-centric view of, 10
    nature of, 10

vaccines, 3, 65, 67
values, 56, 58, 69
    disagreement over, 12

liberal, 104, 108
    religious, 60, 79, 84, 88
vanity, 11
Venn diagram, 109
Virginia, University of, 94
voting, 5, 29, 53, 83, 86–87, 92, 120,
    123

war, 108
Washington, DC, 30–31, 34, 37
Watergate scandal, 84
wealth, 90, 99, 116
Welch, Edgar, 30–31, 34, 37–39
white supremacy, 120, 132, 147–48,
    151
Wikipedia, 103
Williams, Bernard, 177
wisdom, 140
    path to, 11, 142
Wittgenstein, Ludwig, 52–53, 54, 61,
    145–46, 182
women:
    black, 109, 112
    harassment and sexual assault of,
        20, 114, 115, 119, 160
    male power over, 114, 135
    pregnancy of, 113–14
    status of, 87, 88–89
    stereotypes of, 17–18
work, 60
worldview, 61
    arrogance about, 6, 10, 12, 21–23,
        52, 98, 149
    change of, 10, 52

Yale University, 66, 97
Yeats, William Butler, 54

zealotry, 11
    religious, 13

About the Author

Michael Patrick Lynch is Board of Trustees Distinguished Professor and director of the Humanities Institute at the University of Connecticut, where he also leads Humility & Conviction in Public life, a research and engagement project aimed at renewing public discourse. His previous books include *The Internet of Us* and *True to Life*, an Editors' Choice of the *New York Times Book Review*. He lives in Mansfield, Connecticut.